T0072520

THE PATH TO
AWAKENING

Directives from the Divine Council of Light

Book 1

M.V.RAYHN

BALBOA.PRESS

A DIVISION OF HAY HOUSE

Copyright © 2020 M.V.Rayhn.

All rights reserved. No part of this book may be used or reproduced by any means, graphic, electronic, or mechanical, including photocopying, recording, taping or by any information storage retrieval system without the written permission of the author except in the case of brief quotations embodied in critical articles and reviews.

Balboa Press books may be ordered through booksellers or by contacting:

Balboa Press
A Division of Hay House
1663 Liberty Drive
Bloomington, IN 47403
www.balboapress.com
844-682-1282

Because of the dynamic nature of the Internet, any web addresses or links contained in this book may have changed since publication and may no longer be valid. The views expressed in this work are solely those of the author and do not necessarily reflect the views of the publisher, and the publisher hereby disclaims any responsibility for them.

The author of this book does not dispense medical advice or prescribe the use of any technique as a form of treatment for physical, emotional, or medical problems without the advice of a physician, either directly or indirectly. The intent of the author is only to offer information of a general nature to help you in your quest for emotional and spiritual well-being. In the event you use any of the information in this book for yourself, which is your constitutional right, the author and the publisher assume no responsibility for your actions.

Any people depicted in stock imagery provided by Getty Images are models, and such images are being used for illustrative purposes only. Certain stock imagery © Getty Images.

Print information available on the last page.

ISBN: 978-1-9822-5197-0 (sc)
ISBN: 978-1-9822-5199-4 (hc)
ISBN: 978-1-9822-5198-7 (e)

Library of Congress Control Number: 2020913830

Balboa Press rev. date: 09/12/2020

DEDICATION

For the collective

CONTENTS

FOREWORD

**From Archangel Michael, supreme destroyer,
grand council leader, right hand of God**

This book is designed to spark recognition and awaken who you are—who you really are. It goes without saying the 3D identity you have lived, consciously and unconsciously, was chosen by your soul, your oversoul, your highest expression of you, and God. However, you have lived unconsciously for far too long, hindering the growth of your soul, and more importantly, hurting, polluting, and cancering Gaia, the nucleus and epicenter of the intergalactic community. Because of your unconscious, blind following of 3D human rules that were falsely given to you, your soul's compass and remembrance lens are askew. This book and these words serve the purpose of awakening within your soul, your DNA, and your soul map who you really are, who your soul is, and why you are here—here, there, and everywhere. Most importantly, this book will show you your role in awakening the rest of humanity, ushering in the end times of the false 3D collective programming, and beginning the New Age, the new earth, and the healed Gaia. Heed these words, and your soul will rise and ascend and realign to its highest purpose, the Godhead energy, and the Christ energy. You are not here to slumber through existence like unconscious drones. You are *all* here with purpose—the most important purpose: *to awaken yourselves to the truth. And to save Gaia.*

INTRODUCTION

My relationship with angels began right when I was born. My father loved to tell me how my grandfather took my name, birthday, and birth time to their Buddhist monk for a fortune assessment. The Buddhist monk said, "She is the child of angels and cannot be touched. Raise her with care. She is smart but is extremely stubborn." Over the years, he would often quote these wise words, using them as sardonic quips if I was misbehaving or proud exclamations if I was succeeding. It always stuck with me, "Child of angels." At the time it felt more like an incorrect language translation or just a playful metaphor because angels couldn't possibly exist.

God, goddess, the angels, and the universe have quite the sense of humor. Sometimes they speak in vague riddles, subtle signs, or loud slap-across-the-face "aha!" moments. But they also can be very literal at times—too literal for my stubborn nature to accept. That is, until Archangel Michael revealed himself to be my divine guide. This was before I understood the language of synchronicity and how divine messages came from everyone and everywhere. That's when I learned angels were not just fluffy, invisible, cherubic myths from religious texts. They were far advanced light beings in a civilization beyond what human minds were able to comprehend. And while this divine truth defied existing angelic knowledge and lore, it was undeniable how comfortably it rested in my soul.

Growing up in a blue-collar, immigrant family, my existence was grounded in 3D human programming. Learning to work. Working to live. Enjoying the mini moments in between. I was a mundane, with no extraordinary, supernatural abilities. At most, I had a strong intuition for milestone decision making that ironically failed to work with romantic relationships and the occasional, everyday bad choice.

There were multiple cycles that appeared in my life that at the time felt dark, evil, and negative, but now in hindsight, they were necessary.

They were human trials and lessons of releasing and healing shame, unworthiness, anger, depression, disease, abandonment, fear, and all the big and small traumas in between. With each emotion came a cycle that lasted a few years. And by the end of each emotional lesson, more of an extrasensory ability emerged, including: awareness of angels; synchronicities; sequential angel numbers; unconscious astral travels; prophetic visions in dreams; spirit animal visits; seeing nonhuman entities; and acceptance of *being* an angel living a human experience.

In sleep, I astral traveled often. On too many occasions, I felt the real me shake off my human skin suit and fly away on a new adventure. I went to a new place, away from Earth and the taint of humans. It wasn't until a guided meditation class in 2018 that the conscious astral traveling began. Put under a hypnotic trance, and feeling my consciousness release, I traveled to other dimensions. The first trip I made was "home." This home was a state of pure bliss and love, situated atop a mountainous cliff that overlooks an ocean, surrounded by lush, rolling hills. When I arrived, I ran through the grassy fields with glee and utter joy. Happiness filled my soul, and the peace that suffused my being was like none other.

Every Wednesday at the guided meditation class, I tried to return to this happy place that felt like home. Then on one occasion, a black panther spirit guide appeared. Sensing he wanted me to follow him, I ignored the summons, wary and afraid. I left "home" and ended up in a Fae pond, with colorful magical fairies bobbing on lily pads and sprinkling the air with glitter. It was lovely and I wanted to stay, until he became impatient and grabbed my wrist, dragging me to a golden temple.

The golden temple appeared in the middle of a vast desert, with white and gold sand and small patches of grass dotting the horizon with green splashes. Black panthers lazed and slowly meandered around the temple peaks. Walking in, a woman appeared, her face unclear, tall, lithe, wearing a long white gown, with a round, iron-colored head dress.

"Mother," spilled from my lips unconsciously, as if from my

soul's memory. She handed me a gift. I began to cry, and she gently kissed each cheek tenderly. Stepping outside the temple, my feet met the white and gold sand. The atmosphere, sky, and ground began to change. Cycles of birth, growth, and death reeled one after another.

I was confused by the vision and tucked it away into a tell-all-tomorrow bucket for my friends. After I left class, the urge to take out a piece of paper and write was *so* strong. I followed my intuition. I lit a white candle, and the words emerged from an unknown entity and place. They poured forth, and the pen didn't stop writing. It was as if another consciousness was conversing with my consciousness *inside* my mind, accompanied with full seeing, hearing, and feeling sensations. At first it began as one word dribbles, then short sentence flows, and then, as my mind, body, and spirit could handle more, it became paragraph and page tsunamis. This new ability turned my well-structured 3D life upside down. And yes, I feared that my mind was breaking grew. Our society is unkind to those who are different. I was blessed and grateful that God, Goddess, Archangel Michael, and the universe sent me a group of beautiful women, all magical with strong, intuitive gifts, who helped me through this. I am beyond grateful for all of them, as it took me some time to become comfortable and confident with not just the ability to channel but also with the slew of other nonhuman gifts that came with it. It was almost as if a long-forgotten door in my soul swung open, with a loud, "*Remember.*"

The integration of these paranormal abilities was soul-crushingly difficult at its worst and soul bliss at its best. All throughout the journey, I meticulously wrote down each and every transmission, word for painstaking word, and didn't realize until a year later, after twelve journals, that these were for the collective and meant to be shared.

As this is book one, Archangel Michael and the divine were *very* specific on what was to be included and what was not. Their words and this journey have changed my mind, body, spirit, and soul so much that the old *me* is someone I couldn't go back to if I tried. I hope these words bring you the same amount of soul impact they did me so you also remember who you really are.

Considerations

All "you" references address humanity as a collective whole.

All date and time mentions are accurate and were left in as instructed by the divine. Also when human 3D dates are mentioned here, they indicate a beginning of events. What timeline, dimension, vibration, frequency, and reality level they are were not fully disclosed to me. If that event occurs at the highest possible timeline, dimension, vibration, frequency, and/or reality, how and when it manifests or trickles down into 3D is to be determined.

CHAPTER 1

Remembering All of the *Mes*.

The path to awakening begins with remembering who we are.

October 15, 2018

Dispelling Fear

Archangel Michael: Believe with the heart. Accept with the soul.

October 22, 2018

The Divine Mother Introduces Herself

Me: Divine Mother, are you a seraphim?

Divine Mother: Yes, child. I am.

Me: Divine Mother, can you tell me about you?

Divine Mother: What is there to tell? I am your Divine Mother—
to you and to many. I've watched, nurtured, guided, loved,
chastised—gently, of course—cried, celebrated, and rejoiced as
any proud parent would.

Me: Divine Mother, I don't know what to say.

*I can see and feel her smiling warmly. I cannot make out the details
of her face, but I know she's doing it.*

Me: I'm still a little tongue-tied and in shock. You don't have ten eyes
and six wings as all the legends say seraphim do.

Divine Mother: This is just one of my forms, the one your human
mind can handle for now. My true form, I show no one. They
are not ready. I do not wish to hurt you. Those who interpreted
me and us did so with loose imagination and inaccuracy. The
human mind is not yet vast enough to comprehend us. For now,
let's say I am made of light and love. All light and love. The
source is the light and love of me. I am a feminine divine power,
so you may think of me as a mother. Your mother. I've watched
over you all since you were a seedling of light. Your awareness,

3

your soul, your light, your being, and your love expand and expand the universe, stretching it to possibilities that are vast.

Me: I'm not sure what to say. I'm in shock. What am I doing here?

Divine Mother: Our work—the work of the almighty goodness and that which is light and love. Creation is created with love. Only love. Follow your soul's path—the path I set for you all. The path your father set for you all. The path that you set. It leads to love. It is love. Shine bright every day. Be an example through the darkness. Be the light that dispels darkness. You all have done so by your own might. You will do so for others. Do so for others. They need it. All my children need it. You all will lead them. Think beyond the human construct. Think beyond possibilities that not yet are, for that is where this planet and its toxic energy need to go. We have hope. No, we know, the (*she pauses here, searching for the right words. Instead, she shows me planet earth, and there is a viscous, membranelike, black stickiness coating the planet*) … web and tackiness of filth will be disintegrated from the planet's sphere/aura once it ascends. That is our divine plan. We will see it so. You all will/must assist. You all are already doing so. I will lift the veil slowly to you. But I will do it slowly, over time. Trust and believe. Remain in gratitude.

Me: Is that allowed, Divine Mother? (*Lifting the veil.*)

Divine Mother: There is no allow/not allow; it just is as I will make it so. Be at ease. I know the heart of hearts. Trust in your Divine Mother.

Me: Why have you waited so long to reveal yourself?

Divine Mother: Be at peace, as I made it so. We will have eternity together. Human years are inconsequential.

October 26, 2018

The Council and Call to Arms

Divine Mother: We have a lot to discuss.

Me: Divine Mother, I'm scared.

Divine Mother: There is nothing to fear, child.

(*The Divine Mother is standing in the middle of a pyramid, glowing gold and fiery like the sun. I've never seen her this bright yet since she's appeared to me.*)

Divine Mother: Come closer.

(*I'm standing on the sand, looking up at the pyramid.*)

Divine Mother: Do not be afraid.

(*The pyramid is now hollow in the middle with no walls, just steps leading up to a dais-like platform. The pyramid top is still there. One by one, other fiery gold and sunlike figures appear in pairs, standing together on each side of the pyramid. There are eight in total. They shine so bright, like mini suns at high noon.*)

Council: Don't be afraid. You know who we are. You know who you are. Kneel, child. You've done wrong, but with good intentions. For that we forgive.

Me: I am sorry, Divine Mother. I am so sorry.

Council: Do not fret, child. You are not on trial.

(They laugh.)

Me: I am sorry for the wrong I've committed.

Council: We tease, child. *(They shine brighter as they laugh.)* We can still be amused. We have not forgotten how to laugh and be playful. Do not fear us. We are the council. Hello, our child. Our child of light. We came to see your evolution and progress. We are indeed amazed and proud. You all bring us proudness, as all parents feel with a successful child.

Me: I'm sorry, but I'm not sure what to say.

Council: Ask us why we are here.

Me: I'm afraid to.

(They laugh.)

Council: We will share the reason why. It is time for judge, jury, and execution. Destroyers all will be activated. It is time to cleanse the earth, and you all will help, as your souls signed on to do.

Me: I'm sorry, I don't remember anything.

Council: Shall we remind/show you?

(They show me twelve destroyers hovering above the planet, floating in space. They are all wearing armor. There is a combination of females and males. Everyone is carrying something in their hand. There are different types of staffs. A gold light starts at the North Pole and coats the earth, incinerating/wiping everything and the planet clean until there is nothing but a blank white slate.)

Council: There are twelve safety/precautionary measures if ascension does not work. We can undo any that were started. If the creatures on this planet poison the soul of this planet again, reassessments will be made, and species will be purged to start anew.

Me: I thought you were waiting for the humans to evolve and ascend the planet themselves?

Council: Yes. Original, updated, optimized plan. All plans diverge, as do fate lines. The course of this planet is no different. Countermeasures are enacted for alternative pathways in lines of advancements. Just as human souls create alternative pathway lines, so will this planet.

Me: What will happen to us?

Council: This is for judgment, jury, and execution of only those who are damned and unworthy of redemption. Every creature and thing, regardless of its origin, will be judged if it resides on this planet that we, the council, have reset multiple times prior. The race of humans is yet to prove salvageable. If not, we will architect anew—better, unflawed, impervious to poison and toxic darkness. We are disappointed with the results. Unlearned carcasses are of no use for evolution. The time is now. Our patience wears thin. We see all, and what we see is destruction.

(They show me earth. All the wars and violence dotting the surface cause black, sooty smoke to smear the planet like black bruises. This was different from what the Divine Mother showed me in another vision. She showed me the auric field of planet earth, and that was also coated in black, viscous, tarlike muck.)

Council: Our creation is dying. It is sick—soul sick. We will purge the disease if it cannot integrate peacefully [*meaning humans*]. This has been the worst chapter but the most hopeful. We took the biggest chance [*implying biggest risk they took*]. But patterns repeat, and salvation is only for those worthy. Do you understand, child?

Me: There is still beauty and good here.

Council: We will quarantine that which is still pure and preserve it. These will be the successes. The failures will be purged.

Me: Divine Mother … Divine Mother …

Divine Mother: Be brave, my child. Be brave. I love you all. Love, light, destruction. That which burns purifies. You *all* will be our flame and purify the earth back to cleanliness. Back to love and origin-source state.

Me: Divine Mother, this is very scary. I don't know what to say.

Divine Mother: Don't be afraid to confront the *you* within.

(*One by one they leave until only the Divine Mother remains, bright auric field dimming. She smiles warmly.*)

Divine Mother: I am still your Divine Mother. There is nothing to fear. You all are the children of my soul. And I will watch over you always, love you and cherish you. I do not give or assign that which can't be handled. You have my strength and love. You all are wise. You all are truth. As am I. You are me; I am you. Creators are we. We were created for balance. To correct imbalances. To enforce balance. All of creation is balanced and harmonious. As is love. Pure love. When that is disrupted time and again, it creates an injustice in the universe. And those who create stains in the fabric of matter that makes up our universe must be punished.

Me: How, Divine Mother? How?

Divine Mother: Listen to your soul and its memory song.

(*She kisses my forehead and each cheek gently, then embraces me.*)

Divine Mother: You all are a gift to me. I love you all. Be well.

(*She turns around and leaves.*)

October 30, 2018

The Ascension Pace Is Too Slow

Me: Archangel Michael, are you there?

Archangel Michael: Yes, child.

Me: Archangel Michael, can you tell me what/how/when of this destroyer business? I can't remember.

Archangel Michael: I will not share details, as they will derail you and obsess your mind unnecessarily.

Me: Is it going to happen in my current incarnation?

Archangel Michael: Yes.

Me: Will it be fire? Brimstone? Destruction like in the movies?

Archangel Michael: Yes and no. It will occur inside this veil, yes. No other systems will be affected.

Me: Will the humans know it's happening? Or is it a behind the scenes type thing?

Archangel Michael: Both. The planet and its people will know judgment, jury, and execution have arrived.

Me: Are you going to send spaceships like in the movies? Where angry aliens bomb everything?

Archangel Michael: No flying apparatuses will be used. *(He looks amused.)*

Me: I just want to know if the humans will know it's judgment season. Or will it be anticlimactic and behind the scenes?

(While I feel a deep love, affection, and tenderness for both Archangel Michael and Divine Mother, Archangel Michael feels more familiar— like I can be myself with him and not worry about formalities and be silly and playful. As if we have a deeper connection. I feel slightly wary of the Divine Mother, a deep-rooted compulsion to treat her with utmost respect and deference. And I can't be joking with her about humans. It's a similar sensation to having a favorite parent.)

Archangel Michael: Indeed, child, indeed. There are some on the council that wish for a slow ascension, but the decay of the planet cannot handle a slow ascension pace. The timeline has sped up. And now we will force the outcome. Not all council members are in agreement with this. Humans are coddled, poisonous vipers.

Me: Ouch.

Archangel Michael: I pass no judgment. I'm merely stating an observation. They will be fixed. Recycled, rewired, optimized. Architected anew.

Me: That sounds much needed.

Archangel Michael: The multiverses are watching for planet earth's ascension success.

October 31, 2018

The Planet Resets

I received a vision from the Divine Mother. At the end of 2019, I am in my living room. I collapse onto the ground. Humans collapse onto the ground simultaneously, all around the world. The twelve destroyers float or hover around planet earth, pulling all the souls off into their staffs. They appear as gold little balls of light—millions and millions of little gold balls of light. After judgment, they are returned to the creators. Then the destroyers collapse each city, along with each land mass. The planet is wiped clean and reset. The New Earth is created. A state of beauty, pureness and balance. Bright, clear blue skies. White, tufted clouds. Lush greens and rolling hills. Tall trees, swaying in the wind. Warm sun. Paradise. Back to basics. Back to a symbiotic, healthy relationship with Gaia, the planet soul's repaired and healed. The ascended ones are returned here. The destroyers help transition and reintegrate, then leave. Assignment over.

Me: Divine Mother, is what you showed me truth?

Divine Mother: Yes, child, it is.

Me: I saw my body collapsing onto the ground at the end of next year. Is my human coil dying?

Divine Mother: Yes, child. Only your human coil. Yes, that is true.

Me: All souls will be reaped?

Divine Mother: Yes.

Me: I saw all humans collapse at the same time everywhere. And souls were reaped into the staffs of the destroyers and returned into the eyes of the council.

Divine Mother: Yes, that is true. They will be judged, released, and recontracted elsewhere. Those condemned will be punished.

Me: The planet resets, and a small group of humans are resettled?

Divine Mother: Yes, true.

Me: Who are they?

Divine Mother: The ascended ones. Those who helped raise the vibration of the planet will remain on the reset planet, back to its origin state. Their pure souls will live in partnership/balance with the new planet.

Me: Will I get to return to my human coil?

Divine Mother: No, it will be gone.

Me: So I'm dying (my human shell) next year?

Divine Mother: All shells will be punished next year except those worthy and pure, the ascended ones.

Me: What will happen to me then?

Divine Mother: You/they will retain memories so as not to forget, ever again.

Me: There must be another way—an alternative pathway?

Divine Mother: No, there is not. We have analyzed all possible
  pathways. All end in destruction.

  *(I end the transmission with Divine Mother in shock. There's just
so much my human brain can process.)*

November 2, 2018

The Front Line Is Activated

Me: Archangel Michael, are you there?

(My mind meets him at a castle rooftop, where he is gazing up at the stars and an early dawn sky. These are the rooftop castle gardens I've always dreamed of. Now I realize it was a memory. This is how it normally looks to me—smooth rocks are a backdrop to towering walls of water, sourced from origins unknown. Falling peacefully into still streams, they meander throughout pristine marble floors. Lining the pathways, cherry blossom trees bloom, delicate pink, white, yellow, and green petals dotting every surface. Stone arches soar high into the open sky, casting both shadows and illumination. Benches are thoughtfully situated for solitary meditation or group discussion. Occupying every rooftop surface, the gardens instill awe and serenity. But today, no cherry blossoms are in bloom, a signal to Archangel Michael's heavy heart. Only trees are present, their dark green leaves sternly jutting up into the air.)

Me: Can I talk to you again?

Archangel Michael: Of course, child, come sit.

(He pats the seat next to him.)

Archangel Michael: You always come here when your heart is heavy. My heart is heavy too, child.

(He sighs.)

Me: Is everything all right?

Archangel Michael: This isn't something we wanted either. This was our backup plan. While this will be good for all those involved, including our Gaia, the hurt and trauma it will cause humbles us. But it is unfortunately needed, or else it will be too late. Everything will be lost. We showed you all the alternative pathways, and they are all negative. Before your incarnation, there was hope for an outcome according to our plan—that the 1 percent would ascend the humans and the planet. That their high vibration/frequency would serve as a light and love dissemination system and clean up, convert, and raise everyone's vibration through osmosis. Would there still be cleaning up and re-balancing? Yes, of course. As would all ascending planets. But that is not the case. Activating the destroyers is something we did with a heavy heart, as it is now past the original positive outcome juncture into critical destruction territory. And we cannot allow that. The earth, our Gaia, is an important system. It's a nucleus tethering together many systems. It must be saved at all costs. That has always been the priority. Always. Humans were a tool, the means we would use to save our Gaia.

(He looks up at the sky and then down at me. He smiles warmly.)

Archangel Michael: We will give you one human year before enacting judgment. Help raise as many human vibrations/frequencies as possible. One year. You will know, child, how to help those who we put in front of you. Use your eye of judgment to identify the smut on the soul and imbalance of spirit. We have activated all energy healers as well. It is now all hands on deck. The front line is activated—destroyers, healers, preservers, teachers, keepers (of knowledge), truth seers, and soldiers. All were chosen by the council. You all have an important role to play. You will work together to usher in and reset our Gaia. Everyone is important.

Me: Is the timeline fixed for next year? Is that fixed and immoveable?

Archangel Michael: Child, yes. It is so. This is not as bad as your human mind fathoms. Think beyond human construct. The world as the humans know it will change. They did not learn, so we will force it. For those who are deserving, it will be gentle and nondisruptive. They will wake up to a reset Gaia, for all intent and purposes, paradise. All others, depending on their level of frequency, it may or may not be easy depending upon their judgment as a collective whole at that vibration level. Because remember, souls are not sole contributors. They are part and parcel of a larger symbiotic soul ecosystem. They will be judged individually and together. Those at 4D/3D will know, feel, see, hear, and touch a new reality. Everyone will. How painful, severe, and traumatic the judgment and execution will depend on the souls. We will weight it well so they will learn. The 2D and 1D we will destroy. The muck of those levels is too vast and poisonous. We will salvage as much as we can. But they are the levels where the cancer has spread, and they need to be eradicated. They cannot exist any longer. Their energy/vibration is poisoning this universe. That we will not allow.

Me: What happens to me, the destroyers and the front line team you identified?

Archangel Michael: You will all assist the humans in their new realities. Everything they've known will crumble and fall, and new thinking and ways of being must be taught. You all will counsel them. Then you can choose, as they can too, to return home, assignment ended. You may return, of course, as visitors if you so choose.

Me: Is it really only a year?

Archangel Michael: Yes, child.

Me: Is what I saw during meditation class accurate? Are they reaping the souls, returning them back to you and then collapsing the land masses and resetting everything?

Archangel Michael: Yes, child.

Me: Who creates the multiple offset dimensions at the different frequencies?

Archangel Michael: The destroyers with the council's help.

Me: Oh. So this isn't some symbolic, metaphoric, behind-the-scenes spirit, soul, or consciousness change?

Archangel Michael: No, child. For the humans, Gaia, and the planet that you know of as earth this change will be felt at the physical, mental, soul, spirit, and consciousness level of *all*. *All*. change *must* happen for them to learn. There is no other way. We have allowed them their own devices long enough.

Me: How does it work with those incarnated as humans versus those who are native humans?

Archangel Michael: All will be judged, juried, executed, and reaped, regardless of origin.

Me: Okay, I understand.

Archangel Michael: You will do well. I/we love you.

Me: I love you too, Archangel Michael.

Archangel Michael: Be ready. Judgment is here.

Me: One more question. Do we tell everyone?

Archangel Michael: No. That will upset the frequency and spread the cancer/poison. Do not instill fear and panic.

Me: Okay, Archangel Michael. I love you.

November 5, 2018

The Judgment Protocol Is Activated, the Destroyers Are Awake

Divine Mother: Child, come see me. Come to your Divine Mother.

(I travel to her golden pyramid immediately.)

Me: I'm here, Divine Mother. Please tell me what's happening.

Divine Mother: My/our destroyers are awake. Judgment has been set in motion. They were the first to be activated but not the first of events that will occur. They will be the end. We have thinned the veil and allowed darkness in. The giants are awake, as a warning to the humans that their judgment is here. This will be the first in a series of effects till your final judgment.

Me: Divine Mother, please slow down. I need to process.

(Another divine gold light appears in the pyramid.)

Me: Archangel Michael, is that you?

Archangel Michael: Yes, child.

Me: Archangel Michael, what is going on?

Archangel Michael: Judgment protocol has been activated. The humans will understand. Their end is near. They have one year to atone, rise, and improve their frequency. We have unleashed a series of global tests. This the beginning of a segregation of good and bad, light and dark. This is done to test the mettle of souls individually, collectively, and globally as a planet. This is not a pass/fail. This is a filtering or culling of humanity. Who is light? Who is dark? Who is gray?

Me: What do I do?

Archangel Michael: Nothing. Stick with the plan. Help many in the upcoming year.

Me: Is there a way to stop this?

Archangel Michael and Divine Mother (simultaneously): No, child.

Me: What about the destroyers?

Archangel Michael: Not put in motion yet. Awake but waiting. Waiting for our instructions.

Me: I just … keep hoping and thinking there is a better way.

Divine Mother: Child, trust in the council. This is real and happening and unpreventable. We have sent you confirmations and signals. We will do so until you believe.

Me: Please be patient with me. I'm still human with amnesia. This is very hard to process.

Divine Mother: That is changing. We are unlocking your memories slowly. You will believe. This is your soul contract—the plan of seasoned destroyers with a better understanding of doing reapings.

Me: Okay.

Me: Anything else, Divine Mother, Archangel Michael?

Divine Mother: No.

Me: One random question. I read that angels aren't corporeal, just light beings. Does that mean you aren't real? I have memories that you are.

Divine Mother: Child, what humans, other beings, and universes understand of us is very limited. And we make it so. What you know in your heart and soul is true. We are as real to you as your human parents. We are real.

Me: Okay. I love you both. Thank you for the message.

November 8, 2018

The Council Plan Stays the Course

Me: Divine Mother, I'm here.

Divine Mother: Child, let's catch up.

Me: Okay, Divine Mother, what do you want to talk about?

Divine Mother: Be still for now. Rest. Live as a human joyfully as you say. We will summon you when we need you. In the meantime, stick with the plan. Save as many as you can. We will assist if you have questions. But we will leave you be for now, for your mind, body, and spirit to rest. Stay the course. Be brave.

Me: Divine Mother, may I ask a question?

Divine Mother: Yes, go ahead.

Me: Is the timeline still finite? Is it one human year?

Divine Mother: Yes, child. One human year. That has not changed and will not change. Our Gaia must rehabilitate and heal. Our plan stays the course. Our decision is made. Once that is done, there is no moving or changing. Our decision is binding and law.

Me: Okay. So be still. Be patient. Stay the course.

Divine Mother: Yes, child. I love you. Rest now.

Me: I will. Thank you Divine Mother. I love you too.

November 11, 2018

Judgment Is Here and Enacted

Me: Hi Archangel Michael. Happy Sunday.

Archangel Michael: Hello, child. We must talk.

(Archangel Michael appears to me in a friar's brown robe, hands behind his back, looking out the castle windows. This is his war room, where he often carries out angel business. He looks pensive and thoughtful. This is the Archangel Michael I've always known, even before my soul memories unlocked. When I heard and read stories of Archangel Michael as a soft, kind, gentle, guitar-strumming, cherubic divine entity, I laughed. This is the Archangel Michael my soul remembered—intimidating, fierce, mighty, stoic, stern, leader, warrior, but warm, kind, and nurturing. Not everyone gets to see the tough love, playful, mischievous Archangel Michael. Most get the no-nonsense, I command respect, do as I say or else kind of Archangel Michael.)

Archangel Michael: Last night was momentous. It is now my year, and my veil and lock on this earthly plane is unlocked. Judgment is here and enacted. Things will begin escalating quick. Be diligent. Be sharp. Be careful. Stay focused on your assignments and plans. I will create a sacred channel for the destroyers to commune. It's time to prepare.

Me: Can I ask what exactly is supposed to happen now that judgment is here? You're so vague, Archangel Michael. And why are we dropping the veil? Then the neighboring planets will feel and see what's happening here.

Archangel Michael: A few things. Judgment steps natural, environmental, economic, societal, personal, cultural, religious, collegiate/educational, violence/weapons/guns/arms, political, and radical. Old ruins, burials, ancient sites will be unearthed and activated. The humans will know judgment is here. Fear will escalate. Shadows rise. Insecurities heighten. Tempers flare. Then we will see what the humans are made of. Will they make the right or wrong decisions?

Me: This seems so … unethical, unjust, and cruel.

Archangel Michael: This is a culling or filtering.

Me: Did the prior souls who contracted into carnations know there was a possibility of a reaping?

(Archangel Michael looks at me sternly.)

Archangel Michael: Yes.

Me: Oh. What do you want me to do?

Archangel Michael: Nothing. This is an FYI. Information only. Live your life. Continue the mission of saving everyone you can. Sit back and observe. There is nothing for you to do yet.

Me: Can I convince you to optimize, revise, or reverse this plan in any way?

Archangel Michael: No. Our opinions and votes are set. The plan is in motion.

Me: This is cruel to say. But if a year goes by and nothing happens, I'm going to be disappointed.

(Archangel Michael smiles.)

Archangel Michael: Every one, thing, place, event, universe, and galaxy will know and feel this. We will make it so. This is a lesson to all that our Gaia is no longer the unsupervised, liberal, galactic playground or school any more. It is so diseased and unhabitable that it needs to become a soul rehabilitation before anything else. Before any paradise can even be considered, stick with the plan.

November 14, 2018

New Earth Vision

It's Wednesday evening. After work I travel through rush-hour traffic for meditation or astral projection class. The group of people I've met through these sessions are such lovely human beings. The moderator, in particular, is such a gentle and kind soul. It was because of these classes that my abilities started opening up. I owe a huge amount of gratitude to this organization and these wonderful spirits. All are doing positive work for the divine.

I went into class without an intention or motivation to see, hear, or feel any specific thing. I surrendered into what the Divine Mother and Archangel Michael wanted to show. I asked for their help in guiding me. My one caveat was to keep it grounded in positivity. My amnesiac human mind can only take so much fire and brimstone before it descends into anxiety.

The moderator begins class with an essential oil, a prayer, and gentle music. Her voice is so angelic and divine, and it immediately soothes and hypnotizes. Below are the visions the Divine Mother and Archangel Michael showed me.

***

The Divine Mother is there, and I grab onto her hand. She must have felt my rising nervousness because her first words were, "Don't be afraid." She knows me well. We go to her sacred space, where the golden pyramid is. It's a hotbed of activity. Whereas before it was empty, with only black panthers lazing about, now all the destroyers are there, situated around a circular table. There are assistants helping each destroyer, running back and forth bringing books, files, or documents that are scattered all around the table. The destroyers are intensely conversing with each other. I am standing and walking around, writing things on what seem to be blackboards. There are a *lot* of blackboards, lined up in rows like stacked bookshelves. I understand. This is the war room. They are planning out what New Earth is going to look like—what to keep, what not to keep, what to rebuild, etc. I can't escape conference rooms and meetings even in my divine carnation. My speculation is that each destroyer is responsible for one aspect of the rebuild, perhaps an area of expertise. They then make collective decisions and agreements together on outcomes. This makes sense because in my dreams, I have conversations with people, and I wake up not remembering. But every so often, traces of the topic come through. For example, the other morning I woke up, and Rome was on my mind. Rome? What the heck? Now I know.

Divine Mother and I leave the sacred space. She leaves me. Beautiful, scenic views flash by. Autumn leaves. Snow-capped mountains. Serene lakes. Sandy deserts. Rolling, grassy hills. Flower-filled fields. On and on they go, like a slideshow. Are these all the things we will be keeping or replicating? They must be.

Divine Mother then shows me New Earth. The oceans are still there, except they are bluer and clearer than they've ever, ever been. The land masses are all connected again, except they wrap around planet earth like a U. The land looks pristine like a white, sandy palette—a clean slate.

It then flashes to front liners traveling, walking, or riding on horses and wagons to other areas and territories, checking in on how everyone is transitioning. This must be when they make rounds as healers.

It then flashes again to me and a few front liners and destroyers. We travel on horseback to a cave. They are all armored up. It must be a portal. We descend to the other dimensions. This must be us patrolling as a team. New earth seems to be 5D. We bypass 4D, which seems to be what planet earth looks like now, just nicer, and still filled with humans. Perhaps it's the dimension where we leave those who are more light than gray. We end up in 3D. It's not good.

We land where my home is now. And there are zombie-like/demon creatures littered about the streets. Eeesh. The destroyers reap 3D and collapse it. They must have left it for a short period of time for those who needed to be punished. We travel down to 2D, and it's an even darker place than 3D. It's what planet earth looks like now, just dark, decayed, and destroyed by apocalypse. They reap 2D and collapse it. We leave 1D. That's a heavily guarded soul jail. We travel back. I have free will to travel wherever. I spend time alternating between other lands and New Earth, until everything and everyone is situated.

The front liners are seen planning, alternating between each other's homes. As more front liners are activated, the rooms get more filled with people.

It then flashes to a large auditorium or gymnasium. A school auditorium or gymnasium perhaps? There's a lot of people there. Other angels in silver armor are there guarding it. There's a large circle, diagram, or pentagram of some sort on the ground. There are people situated at certain points around the circle. The destroyers are floating above planet earth. We feed the circle's energy into the destroyers, and they aim it at each continent, one at a time. So this is our hail Mary throw, raising the vibrational frequency of each continent.

It then flashes to me sitting on my couch. I get up and collapse onto the ground. And the reaping begins. The destroyers do so with humanity, kindness, and gentleness to protect the souls from trauma. Before they collapse each city, they do so with reverence and gratitude, as they all incarnated here. They walk the streets before doing anything, cataloging places of happiness and memories.

Before I realize it, the moderator pulls us out of meditation, and the visions ends.

December 7, 2018

Thirteen Reapings Too Many; Gaia Is Dying

Me: I'm sorry, go ahead Divine Mother. *(I put her on hold while I grab my journal.)*

Divine Mother: My dearest child, the key difference between the last destroyer assignment and this upcoming is Gaia. The last time a team was sent to Gaia it was to correct the darkness and corruption permeating human coil souls. An aftereffect of that, a byproduct, is a residual stained Gaia, but it did not disease her. At that interval of existence, the humans still respected my Gaia. While their souls were descending into dark, low-frequency territory, they still had not lost their respect or programming *to* respect the land from which they resided. That is the key difference. The darkness, stain, and shadow has destroyed the purity of my souls and my Gaia, causing her disease, illness, decay, and a slow, painful, deteriorating death, where she is rotting in small sections or areas at a time.

Gaia is there in a female form. She projects herself with pieces of flesh missing. Half her face is gone, exposing a skeleton. Large patches of skin are missing on the other side of her face. Open sores and rot are exposing bone are all along her neck, shoulders, arms, and legs. Her heart is exposed, her chest cavity broken into, her rhythm slow. Her core and midsection are also exposed, with her entrails falling out.

Me: OMG, Gaia. Divine Mother.

Divine Mother: Do you see? Do you understand now when I say that Gaia is sick and she must be rehabilitated?

Me: I do, Divine Mother. I do. Oh my Gaia. I am so, so sorry this was done to you. So, so sorry. If I contributed to it in any way by being in this coil, I am so, so sorry. I make a vow to you to do everything in my power to heal you and to punish every single place, person, event, and thing that did this to you. I promise you this.

(Gaia has tears in her eyes. I hug her again gently because she is so frail.)

Me: The keeper crystals are planetary Band-Aids, aren't they?

Divine Mother: Yes, child.

Gaia (simultaneously): Yes. *(Pained whisper.)*

Me: Crap. Sorry don't mean to curse. Divine Mother, may I ask how many times they've reaped Gaia?

Divine Mother: Twelve. This will be thirteenth and the last, my child. It is thirteen times too many. We are putting safeguards and a new plan in place to prevent this from happening—to prevent Gaia from ever getting this sick again. This cannot and this will not happen again.

Me: Is this the first time Gaia has been this sick and was dying?

Divine Mother: Yes. The previous times it was soul corrections, human coil corrections, evolution corrections, and course to ascension corrections. Gaia, my Gaia, was always strong, pulsating bright, like the way I made her. At most, minor injuries and bruises were what she sustained. Now it is different, and the human vermin will pay. They have not learned, yet again. Again.

We have given thirteen opportunities. Thirteen. Thirteen too many. We will reward those who ascended and those who are pure. All else who contributed to disease-ing, killing my Gaia, will pay. The method, how severe, how kind, the process, and the final decisions were a laid-out plan, approved by me and the council. That plan is being enacted now and is a good one.

Me: Thank you so much for the kind words, Divine Mother. I love you. I miss you.

Me to Gaia: I miss you and love you, Gaia.

December 12, 2018

Your Soul Must Be Clear

Me: Hi, Archangel Michael.

(He smiles. He appears to me on the castle rooftop again, sitting on a bench, looking up at the starry night sky. He pats the empty seat next to him.)

Archangel Michael: Come sit, child. I wish to speak with you.

Me: Okay. I'm here.

Archangel Michael: I know it has been difficult. More old traumas will continue to release. We are getting you ready and ensuring your soul is clear and no stains or shadows exist to corrupt the love, light, peace, joy, good, Source, God/universe, Christ, and consciousness energy. You have always been and remain a pure soul, even with all the hurts and trials you have endured, but this cleanse was put in place to ensure your imperviousness to darkness, shadows, and stains.

Archangel Michael: We are prepping you for the upcoming year. Your soul must be clear. We need pure, cleansing, purifying energy to help heal and rehabilitate Gaia. We cannot risk injuring her further. That's why you, your mind, your soul, your body, and your spirit need to be clear, balanced, and unmarked, in order to protect Gaia.

Me: Okay, Archangel Michael. Anything else?

Archangel Michael: Just that I love you, how proud I am of all of you, and how when you are hurting, we all are. Know that we are always watching over you.

Me: Thank you, Archangel Michael. I love you.

Archangel Michael: And I you. And I you. Be well.

CHAPTER 2

The Collective Awakens.

Rise and Awaken.

December 29, 2018

The Timeline Has Moved Up

Me: Yes, Archangel Michael.

(Archangel Michael is in his war room, looking out a window, arms behind him.)

Archangel Michael: How are you?

Me: I'm fine. How are you?

Archangel Michael: Busy. The timeline has moved up. The destroyer assignment will be occurring ahead of schedule.

Me: Okay. When? Although your dates and times seem to vary differently than the human timeline, especially in 3D.

Archangel Michael: It will be early fall of 2019. It is no longer end of your human year 2019 and early 2020.

Me: What about all the soul quotas for New Earth/5D?

Archangel Michael: We will meet our quota. I have teams in place to ensure that part of the plan is met successfully. Ask me.

Me: What about the mission and the horsemen?

Archangel Michael: All are still happening, within an accelerated timeframe.

Me: Okay.

(He's looking at me intently.)

Archangel Michael: I know it has been difficult. Very difficult. We acknowledge that. You are all doing well.

Me: All right, accelerated timeline. What am I supposed to do with this knowledge?

Archangel Michael: Nothing. You will stick with the intended plan. There is no change in your role/assignment.

Me: Thank you for letting me know.

(He's still staring at me intently.)

Me: Why are you looking at me like I have five heads?

Archangel Michael: Technically you have many heads because of all your manifestations, splintered across the multiple dimensions and timelines. Child.

Me: Yes?

Archangel Michael: We will help release the heaviness and tension and anxiety.

Me: Thank you for the help.

Archangel Michael: We know you all have been struggling. We acknowledge and see this. We are helping you, as parents do out of love. Not because this is part of your collective mission or assignment. We are all concerned and worried.

December 30, 2018

We Are Not Gods and Goddesses

Archangel Michael: We are not perfect, but we are your divine guides and parents, and we love you all more than you know.

Me: I thought gods and goddesses were all knowing and impervious to flaws. Everything happens for a reason and nothing by chance or impervious perfection.

(He smiles.)

Archangel Michael: We are not gods and goddesses. We are creators, destroyers, and overseers of all. We just are, child. Nothing is perfect but also perfect all at the same time. That is the beauty in all that is. Because if everyone, thing, place, and event was perfect, how could it evolve and grow. We always create and ensure a level of flaws or an infinitesimal opportunity to improve and evolve and get better. Nothing is perfect, and it shouldn't and doesn't have to be.

Me: That just got super deep, Archangel Michael.

(He smiles.)

Me: Thank you for all of the blessings and abundance in our lives. Thank you for being our divine guardian.

Archangel Michael: I love you too, child.

January 1, 2019

Hello Highest Me of Me

Me: Hello me of me.

(The Divine Mother, higher me, and I are at the golden temple. Higher me towers and smiles down at me warmly. Higher me grabs my hands.)

Higher Me: Do not be afraid. Do not be afraid of that which is foreign and different and outside the constructs of our human minds. I/we have designed our/your human experience and incarnation to be this way and for us to experience everything you are experiencing to learn, evolve, grow, heal again, release into love, forgive, and ascend for reintegration.

(Higher me embraces me warmly and holds onto my hands)

Higher Me: What you/we are experiencing in that incarnation is a manifested copy of our old and deepest soul traumas to approach and heal and release in a different way. This will help us purge the stains and scars once and for all, leaving only gratitude and love and knowledge from difficult earned trials. We are healed from all this. But we know that some traumas burrow deep, and this incarnation was an opportunity to relook, reassess, and reheal from a different manifested perspective. While the circumstances and players were different, the emotions and barriers to heal were the same. We are close—so close—to releasing all the old hurts. Allow us to, for we must to successfully complete this mission and rehabilitate Gaia. Our soul must be clear once again and healed if we are to assume our highest self and abilities for the fulfillment of this assignment. Do not be afraid. Do not doubt us. In our soul, we know truth and what really is. Do not listen to fear.

Me: So the destroyer assignment is real? The reality that is human 3D is ending? And by 2019?

Higher Me: Yes, me of me. You know this to be true. Do not doubt the knowledge of our soul and vast experience. There is a lot to be done while we are in the human incarnation. We must raise our vibration and frequency, inspire others to do so, and ascend as many souls as possible, all while clearing and healing our soul traumas and stains to prepare it for a happy, love-filled, light-filled, peace-filled existence. The time, opportunity, and emergency have arrived to heal, to rehabilitate, to create in love, light, peace, joy, and all that is good, and to be impervious and protected from darkness, evil, and negativity and most of all corruption. These are the cancers and illnesses that are poisoning and harming Gaia, which is also spreading to the multiverse, multigalaxies, and beyond. We will course correct and rebuild a new for a light-, love-, peace-, and joy-filled existence, hopefully until there is no more and beyond. This is not something done often or lightly. It will be done once, well, and will never have to be done again. Gaia can only withstand so many destroyer assignments before she will no longer exist. That cannot happen, the me of me, as you know. So the plan the council laid out, that will be exacted, is a good one, complex and intricate, with a lot of data, truths, knowledge, and expertise. It was developed by a supreme and divine collective of good, blessed by the council and overseen, supervised, and executed by the destroyers. It will be done one final time and never again, leaving Gaia whole, rehabilitated, healed, and safe. Believe and trust in the plan constructed.

Higher Me: Archangel Michael and the Divine Mother are our divine parents, creators, and nurturers. They are made from love, light, good, and divine energies and powers only grounded in all that is good. They love all very much, and they care, watch over us, and protect us very much. Do not doubt them.

(Higher me smiles.)

Higher Me: They are good, true, and made of love and light, and their intentions toward us is always good, true, and grounded in love and light.

Me: All right. Thank you. Anything else to tell me?

(Higher me hugs me.)

Higher Me: You are doing well, me of me. You/we are brave even though it is not always apparent. You/we are wise, kind, and made from love/light. Do not forget that. Breathe and surrender into truth and faith and all that is good.

January 17, 2019

Gaia Returns to the Intergalactic Center

Me: Archangel Michael, are you there?

(Archangel Michael smiles. He's sitting in a sunroom, surrounded by glass and steel windows. Lush foliage is strategically positioned throughout, creating a greenhouse atmosphere. He is drinking something leisurely. Bright sunshine and a clear sky warm the room like a welcoming hug.)

Me: Is this in your castle?

Archangel Michael *(smiles)*: Of course. Come sit.

Me: Are you well?

(I join him at a wrought iron table with matching chairs.)

Archangel Michael: I am. How are you, child?

Me (I smile): I am well.

Archangel Michael: As for your assignment, we've allowed you this time to relive and release the remaining soul memories and traumas and stains. Your jobs there are now complete. Your human assignment of purging and releasing soul memories and traumas is now complete. Moving forward, your focus will be in preparing for the next phase of the destroyer plan or protocol. And that is to prepare for the reaping, as for the horsemen program known as war. He will come on the blood moon.

Me: I want to ask. Why do you keep natural disastering California and Asia?

Archangel Michael: Very good question. Those are land masses that sit on Gaia's energy lines and pathways. We are shifting the land masses slowly, in order to realign the poles to the planetary portals. Once the destroyer protocol is complete, Gaia will be moved back into intergalactic orbit and no longer isolated from all else. She will be a part of the intergalactic community once again—not too close, as she still needs to adjust from the rehabilitation but close enough to not be segregated.

Me: That's what I thought. You're going to tow her back to the center essentially, right?

Archangel Michael (nods): Yes, if you want to use crude human vernacular to describe a divine ascension, sure.

Me: Thank you, Archangel. Oh, one more thing. What happens to the souls?

Archangel Michael: They will get judged and reassigned to new assignments if they have karmic lessons to learn. If they are close to completing their lessons, it will be up to the destroyers if they will pass and go home or be put back into the new systems and rotations. It will be up to the destroyer team what happens to the souls, how gentle, how difficult, how painful, how merciful, how kind the experience. That part of the plan comes after. For now, focus on the next phase of this mission/plan.

Me: Okay, thank you. I love you.

Archangel Michael (winks): Have a good day, child.

Me: Thank you, Archangel Michael. You too.

February 7, 2019

A Destroyer Reaches Out

Destroyer: The timeline is fixed. Gaia will be rehabilitated. Before she is, this planet will be reaped for the final time. That assignment is firm, final, and unmoving. That is also a final and firm decree from the council. Gaia, the human experiment, and the souls inhabiting the avatars will be destroyed and the souls weighed and measured and judged and redistributed. That is still happening.

Me: Archangel Michael and Divine Mother said at the end of the human year 2019. Right now it's February 2019. So the reset, reaping, judgment, or end of this human existence as we know it will end at the end of this year? Am I right?

Destroyer: Yes, that is correct. 5D has already been formed. The framework and essence of 5D has already been developed. All that is needed are the pure souls to power it and manifest it into solidity and reality. Those important elements are already in place. The New Gaia and higher dimension are already in place. We are in the critical judgment phase, purge phase, trial phase, and reset/reap phase.

Me: Okay. So all this is still happening? Part of me doesn't believe you and believes that you, and all of this, is just a figment of my imagination.

Destroyer (softens with compassion and sympathy): It is real. We are real. This is real. All of it is real. We will keep reminding you of this, as much as you need it.

Me: Yes, please do. Because honestly, nothing seems to be any different.

Destroyer: If truths and synchronicities are what is required, then I/we will help, and send as many as you need.

Me: Yes, please. Send *all* the signs. What should we be doing with our jobs? What should we be doing?

Destroyer: Whatever it is, that will bring you joy. If you wish to remain at your current employment, then do so. And it will be blessed and work out best for you. If you wish to leave, then also do so. And that will be blessed and work out best. It is up to you what you desire. You will manifest, and the divine will help you manifest blessings and abundance no matter where or what you do. Whatever it is you desire, it will be so, and it will be blessed.

Me: So if I desire for this destroyer assignment to not happen, does that mean it will not happen?

Destroyer (shakes head): No. You know that is an untruth. The divine, Father and Mother, and all those watching over you there in that plane of existence will help you live out the remainder of your days content and happy and filled with joy. Whatever path you choose, they will help you. That does not mean that contented existence will negate and cancel out the council-decreed destroyer protocol. You know this to be true. Also, it is not what you truly desire, as you know how sick Gaia is, why she is sick, who should be punished for it, and where justice should be enacted. You know the truth of this already. There is no undoing that which needs fixing. Gaia is past the point of critical damage. This assignment and protocol will not be ceased, no matter what.

Me: Okay, so basically you're telling me to do whatever the heck I want, and it will turn out well, because I and everyone else on this rock are dying in a year?

Destroyer: Not dying. Judged, reaped, and reassigned. This is not a soul destruction. This is a reaping and reassigning assignment. Of course those deemed unsalvageable will need to be revaluated. But this is not a cease, destroy, and abandon or leave protocol. This is a *rehabilitation* protocol. There is a significant difference.

Me: Okay, great.

CHAPTER 3

You Are Here to Complete the Mission of Saving Gaia.

Save Gaia.

Awaken Humanity.

M.V.RAYHN

March 24, 2019

Oh No, Divine Mother

Divine Mother: The upcoming full moons are quite significant. And a key milestone will occur with each new cycle. The upcoming one will focus on ascension into 5D and the overlay of 5D onto 3D, with the beginning collapse of 3D as your incarnations know it. It is the beginning of the correction protocol and the end of the individual and global judgment. The second wave of judgment will occur after correction once the souls have been reaped and disintegrated from their human coils. The human assignments and programs have until the next full moon to pick a side: light or dark. Let's all hope they choose wisely.

Me: Divine Mother, does this mean the world is ending in a month!

Divine Mother: No, it just means the first phase of judgment is closing and the tally of points is closing on that round. Final judgment is an accumulation of light and dark. If we were to use human layman vernacular, debits and credits. So now until the next full moon is when this round of judgment will end, and a new one will begin. Each round is scheduled to narrow and cull down the souls further and further, if that makes sense.

Me: So basically these souls need to pass each round of tests? It's not just a few individualized tests per soul?

Divine Mother: It's that and so much more. There are individual soul tests. There are community soul tests, collective soul tests, and karmic soul tests. There are many layers, and it is very complex. Judgment is in place to determine through exact probability and science and trials on which side of light and dark they will land. And when final judgment assumes, they will be reviewed based on all of their soul credits and debits, passes or fails, etc.

Me: You contradicted yourself, Divine Mother. Sorry, trying to understand. So how many rounds of judgment are there?

Divine Mother: Many. Assume each new moon cycle triggers a new phase of tests until the correction protocol finishes.

Me: So if I'm understanding correctly, each new full moon is a different judgment phase and a new set of tests. And more tests will be introduced to get the souls to pick a side until the final end, which is when final judgment happens.

Divine Mother: That is accurate.

Me: And the collapse of 3D and the human constructs as we know it is a global and collective judgment and test?

Divine Mother: Also accurate. It will trigger many individual and community and collective and global tests. It is an intricate process.

March 27, 2019

No One Is Exempt

Divine Mother: Every one, thing, place, and event is not exempt and never was. Never was this a free pass with no judgment. After the reaping and judgment, all souls will return from whence they came, which means they did *not* come from 5D as 5D is newly formed. If the souls of your loved ones wish or desire to make 5D their new place of residence, then yes, they may go ascend and go there by their own free will versus returning to their origins before their human incarnation. But they must pass judgment. If they do not, depending on their souls' judgment, they will return to their origin location or need to continue on in an alternate rotation to complete the soul lessons.

May 17, 2019

You Will Become *You*

Divine Mother: Continue shedding that which is no longer useful and ascending and de-programming the toxic patterns and behaviors emulsifying and permeating the 3D human construct. You give us hope for the souls for 5D. I/we were becoming concerned we would have to enact the destroyer protocol and reset protocol and rehabilitate protocol without meeting the pure soul quota needed to power 5D. But seeing all of you struggling to slowly break out of your dark, corrupt 3D constructed cocoons brings me hope. We only need a small few for 5D. And that small few is doing well enough that we stay the course.

Me: Okay, sounds good, Divine Mother. No news is good news. Is there anything we should be doing?

Divine Mother: Stay the course. Continue onward, and continue what you all are doing—healing, shedding, ascending, realigning with source, rebecoming your true selves, reintegrating your fractured selves, and loving and living joyfully as you can moment by moment. You are doing well—so well. Keep up the hard but necessary work. We will always watch over, protect, and keep you all safe and continue helping, aiding, and guiding in all the way you need. It is time for 3D, the 3D we have lost to darkness to know their end/destruction is here.

Divine Mother: Do not be afraid. This is a necessary step in this plan. And you all will begin to feel and be much, much better, as you will *be* in line with your true self, your true essence, your true power, your true you. 3D toxins will no longer rule you all.

You will rule them. You will no longer feel fear, the irrational fear that permeates 3D. They will fear *you*. Everyone, everything will now know their end is here, through you all. And they will be afraid—afraid enough to change and to inspire/trigger to be better, to grow, to ascend, to shed, to heal, and most importantly, to wake up from the toxic, corrupt, dark programming.

Me: This sounds a little vague. I'm sorry. Can you help me understand a little more? It sounds like I will be completely different moving forward?

(Divine Mother smiles.)

Divine Mother: You all will be. You all will become your true self.

Me: But isn't my true self a gigantic light blog? Ha, ha. Sorry, my brain is still human 3D.

(Archangel Michael smirks.)

Archangel Michael: You all will feel better, be better. You will be able to do, see, hear, and feel as your true self. You will be you. You will see and know all. You will detach from the 3D construct or program and see 3D as your true self. You will use this gift and enhancement or as human vernacular states, an upgrade to help others, and also to wake up out of the dark. Understand now?

Me: I think so. In full transparency, it is very difficult here. We are all struggling, stumbling around in the dark, not sure of what to do, how to be, filled with negativity but also unsure how to be and live happily/joyfully. It is very hard. I am not complaining, merely explaining how well the poisoned 3D construct has corrupted our view. Everything and everyone is backward. Ha. And we don't remember the *right* way. Ha.

(Archangel Michael and Divine Mother smile.)

Archangel Michael: That is why you all will help the unawakened and poisoned. Be their light. Be their hope. Remind and teach them the right way.

Divine Mother: I, your father, love you *all* very much. Always remember that. Be well. Be happy. Be at peace.

Me: Thank you, Divine Mother. I am grateful. I love you too. Thank you for all of the help and guidance.

M.V. RAYHN

June 21, 2019

Inspiration from Archangel Michael

Stop Trying So Hard. Just Be.

July 2, 2019

The Ships

During a casual reading with a friend, there was an oracle card drawn that said to pay attention to my higher self and spirit guides. Last week something guided me to buy Dolores Cannon's *The Convoluted Universe Book 5*. It's been sitting on my nightstand.

Then last night, I felt a strong pull to pick up that book, as there was a message inside for me. I said a prayer to God/Goddess and Archangel Michael for guidance. I opened it to a chapter, "I Am You," and the content was all about how these two people met higher versions of themselves.

Person one was a woman who met her higher self. While here helping humanity during the shift over the years, more and more of her true self downloaded into her human self. It was a slow integration so her human self wouldn't explode.

Person two was a man on a ship. What stuck out, and the information given to me, was how during our upcoming shift (the ascension, the splitting of timelines, the end, whatever we are calling it) ships—space*ships*—will be arriving to assist with the *shift* and literally take *all* the souls off. I read this and tucked it away, going to bed. It didn't feel immediate.

The next day I got up and went to work, late of course. On the car ride, I kept thinking about why I was awake, and suddenly astral traveling to a *ship* a lot these past few days. And then it *hit* me like a smack in the gut that our ascension is a *literal* ascension … on a *ship*.

We have to raise our frequency to a 5D vibration or else we won't *see* these ships and be able to get on.

I asked Archangel Michael if this was true, and he winked, gave a thumbs up, and gave the universal keep quiet symbol for, "Shhhh."

I then asked God/Goddess for the truth, and they confirmed it was true and that the ships would be here very, very soon.

Their message was very cryptic: "The end is here. We are coming. Stay the course." (Continue soul work and ascending shedding layers.)

Archangel Michael inferred again it was our choice, due to free will, if we decide to stay on the ships or come back.

Something big is definitely happening with these ships.

July 6, 2019

A Divine Feminine Pep Talk

Be well.
Keep going.
You all are brave.
You all are strong.
You all are stronger than you ever realized.
Be happy.
Be joyous.
Be light.
Be love.
Smile.
Just be.
That's all, nothing else … just *be*.

M.V.RAYHN

July 7, 2019

Destroyer Message

Be healthy. Take care of the vessel so it runs optimally, but don't attach to it. It is not really you.

CHAPTER 4

If You Don't Remember, We Will Help You Do So.

Save Gaia.
Awaken Humanity.

September 17, 2019

Mini Bonus Judgment Round

Me: Hi, Archangel Michael.

Archangel Michael: Shall we discuss the next phase of the plan?

Me: Yes, please. I'm ready. I am grateful for any and all information you have to share.

Archangel Michael: The judgment protocol is coming to a close.

(My phone pinged as a confirmation.)

Archangel Michael: The judgment of humanity in 3D is closing, and those who are dark remain in 3D and will be dealt with by the destroyers during the reaping. The destroyers choose how harsh, how easy, and how in-between their judgment, reassignment, and reset will be. They've had their chance to raise their frequency and vibration and awaken to the divine truths of their soul, but they are too weak to overcome and break through. They will be reaped and dealt with first. We have zero tolerance and patience for these dark souls. If they have not passed their judgments, trials, and tests, then their opportunity to rise and awaken to a higher vibration or frequency is lost to them. The council has a no-tolerance policy for failing judgment constituents. Now for gray souls, this is a different matter. They will be issued, let's call it, a mini bonus judgment round, where the judgment, trials, and traumas of the past year will be compounded into a shortened window—a soul trial if you will. We will ignite their gray souls with fire, judgment, and pain and determine which side they will choose. There is a higher-vibrational frequency mired in ego-poisoned human stain. This is a culling. Not everyone, every place, and everything will ascend. You all are on a good path. Continue rising. Continue choosing the ascended path. Continue choosing the divine path of love and light and joy. Remember joy. Release all fear. All negativity. All feelings of lack and unworthiness. All, and I mean all, are 3D ego programming.

Me: How do we do that?

Archangel Michael: Do you think you're out of the gray? Belief is the test. It is as simple as that and yet difficult all at the same time. Belief and trust. Can you all continue to uphold the frequency of belief and trust?

Me: Yes sir! Yes! Always!

Archangel Michael: Good. That's all you need to.

Me: May I ask, what exactly are we believing and trusting?

Archangel Michael: Believing in divine love, light, happiness, peace, and joy. Trusting it exists and surrendering into it. Releasing *all* fear. Conquering the toxic ego monkey mind. Believe, trust, and surrender. It is simple. Believe. Trust. Surrender.

Me: Are we all just epically failing at this?

Archangel Michael: No, I did not say that. All of you are on a good, higher, ascended path. Can you all do better? Yes. So do better. The human construct of time is running out for all of you. It is time to choose divine love, light, peace, joy, and happiness. Our patience runs thin. Very thin. We have culled humanity, and the chosen have emerged and risen. The rest, well ... they are what they are. Continue as you all are. Remember to choose divine love, light, peace, joy, and happiness. Believe. Trust. Surrender. That is *all*. This message is for all those who will read this. This is decreed by the divine council of light, and judgment is now ending. Humanity, if not on the side of divine love, light, peace, and joy, will feel the trauma and the finality of decision in their souls. Choose a path of ascension to divine love, light, peace, and joy. If this message is still unclear to you all, then you will not pass, and your fate will reside with the destroyers. Our patience wears thin.

Me: Thank you, Archangel Michael.

Archangel Michael: Be well. Get ready. The end of 3D is near.

(When this transmission ended, the clock read 11:11.)

September 18, 2019

Good News = A+ Pass

Me: Archangel Michael?

(It's 6:00 a.m. I was summoned by Archangel Michael, when a sliver of me broke off and sat on the edge of my bed. I was awake on the ship, in a bed. I yawned, groggily walking through the ship hallways to the control room. Archangel Michael is standing there with long black robes, hands casually behind his back.)

Me: Hi. Is everything all right?

Archangel Michael: Hello.

(He smiles warmly down at me.)

Archangel Michael: I wanted to share some good news with you.

Me: Okay. I'd love to hear it. Thank you for sharing.

Archangel Michael: I am very proud of you all. We are very proud of you all. What you've shed and accomplished and released and integrated and overcome this past year since this journey has begun has been extraordinary. Job well done. You all healed your shattered and shadowed selves or slivers. You purged your soul of traumas, you healed very old, very deep soul traumas and wounds, you healed and integrated all of your broken slivers, and you unshackled yourselves. You all far surpassed our expectations as I knew you would. You all were always whole and complete and extraordinary but now even more so. You all are a gift to us all. So I wanted to share that you all have passed your soul trials and are free of judgment. You will continue to integrate into your highest self to *become* a *new* version of yourselves. You all will be reborn and rebirthed. You are free. You are whole. You are unbounded and shackle free. You all were tested, trialed, and cleared, and your souls are pure, true, good, and only love, light, and joy. You all are ready for Gaia, and for this next stage, protocol, and plan of the reset. You will start to feel the mind, body, spirit, and soul adjust to the influx of power and energy. As you integrate and ascend, you all will feel it. You—all of the yous—will integrate, and you will become one again, *new* and *rebirthed*, whole and complete once again. Do you understand?

(I look at him, and he's looking at me with warm eyes.)

Me: Thank you for the kind words, Archangel Michael, and for sharing the news. Can I ask a few questions?

Archangel Michael: Of course. Go ahead.

Me: I saw and felt a sliver of me separate from me and sit on the bed. What does that mean? Why am I breaking apart?

Archangel Michael: You are not. There are pieces of you that will break and shed off and reintegrate into you at a higher vibrational or frequency manner. These slivers that no longer serve you will break off, dissolve, and reintegrate back into you as divine love, light, peace, and joy. Do not be alarmed when this occurs.

Me: Okay. That's a relief. When all of the mes integrate, what happens to the sliver of consciousness that is *me*. Do I die? Do I just dissolve and integrate back into higher me? That's a little sad I think.

Archangel Michael: Yes and no. Yes, all of the yous, including your higher self, will dissolve and integrate into one self again, including all of your consciousness. Because you are the *shadow and* the power source of your soul, the pieces of you that dissolve and integrate and rebirth essentially integrate, merge, and fuse into you, the shadow and source of power. Does that make sense? You *are* the soul power, so the pieces of you integrate back into *you*. You will become whole and one once more, balanced in mind, body, spirit, and soul.

(I smile.)

Me: Thank you, Archangel Michael. So what happens now?

(He smiles.)

Archangel Michael: Celebrate.

(He smiles again.)

Archangel Michael: This was no small feat. You all did incredibly well. I am very proud.

Me: Thank you, Archangel Michael.

(I sigh with relief.)

Archangel Michael: Rest these upcoming days. Honor your body. We will begin the integration process, and it will fatigue. Rest. We love you. We are happy and proud of you all.

Me: Thank you.

(I smile.)

Me: May I share this?

Archangel Michael: Yes you may.

Me: Thank you, Archangel Michael.

September 21, 2019

Reset Protocol Begins

.

(Right before falling asleep, I felt myself pulled to a golden temple high in the sky. This one floated in the air among the clouds, open on all four sides. I showed up in the middle, and gold light blobs began emerging, one by one. The council. I heard Archangel Michael say, "You may want to write this down." I was integrating with higher me. It was the first time I became aware of my true form, lying on the bed.)

Me: Hi, Archangel Michael, Divine Mother.

Archangel Michael and Divine Mother *(simultaneously)*: Hello, child.

Divine Mother: We've come with news, updates, and congratulations. We are so proud of you all. If you weren't aware of what transpired these past few human 3D days, it was quite momentous. You all are the first higher dimensional frequency or vibration integration and merged with a 3D ego consciousness. It was quite successful. You all should be very proud of yourselves. Moving forward you are and will be the highest expression of yourself. More memories will unlock. More abilities and skills will unlock. More knowledge, wisdom, and truths will unlock. More awareness, more consciousness, and connected consciousness will unlock and emerge. You all are rebirthing while ascending or rising into 5D and beyond. The old 3D ego self that you've identified with in this human incarnation will die off slowly, so as to not shock the mind, body, and soul, and you all will be born, emerging as a new you. There is nothing to fear. These are all wonderful blessings and gifts and the rewards from all the hard soul work accomplished in this incarnation.

You and those around you will notice a change, transition, and newness about you. Your mind, body, spirit, and soul will change and become the new you over a time, and all who know you will know a new you, a you they've never seen or known before. It is now time for you all to step into your true self. We have given you all ample time to finish your soul work and you've done tremendously—far beyond our expectations. You give us hope for the chosen few who will rise and ascend into Gaia. We will soon begin activating the reset protocols. You will all step into your true selves and assume your mantles of responsibilities. We gave you one human year, and that mile mark is near. We have judged, weighed, measured, and culled out the light, gray, and dark. All have been judged, and it is now time for 3D humanity to know and fully understand their judgment and their results. Our patience and our understanding and compassion are now expired. The reset and punishment will now begin.

Me: Thank you for the update, Divine Mother, Archangel Michael, council. May I ask what happens now?

Divine Mother: You all will continue as you are, choosing, living, and inspiring each other and others of higher frequency or vibrational existence. Regardless of everything, every place, and every event that occurs around you, and know that much will now begin to occur, you are always safe, protected, and shielded. All of you will be safe, protected, and shielded … to a degree. There are some that still waver. Be sure not to waver, and stand firm in happiness, love, light, peace, and joy.

Me: Okay, Divine Mother. We will try. Please be patient with us. We are all trying our best.

Divine Mother: I/we know and understand. We are patient, understanding, and compassionate to those who deserve it.

Those who don't will now know our warnings were not false and humanity and those living in low, unawakened frequencies will understand true fear and the wrath of me and the council. I/we have been patient, kind, and too forgiving for far too long. The destroyers will be readied, and the reset protocol begins. There will be a series of global, collective, large disasters to awaken and force further culling and punishment. Be ready. Do you understand?

Me: I think so.

Divine Mother: 3D humanity is now resetting and reaping. We gave you all ample time. We gave humanity far longer. The reset and reaping begin.

Me: What should we do, and I know time is a false 3D construct, but if you were to guess, when is this happening? This year? Next year? Within the next few years?

Divine Mother: It is the one year mark given earlier. We warned you all. Be ready.

Me: Okay. May I share with the others?

Divine Mother: Yes, you may.

Me: Anymore messages for them?

Divine Mother: Stop wasting effort on 3D human ego rules and programming. These will all be destroyed, reset, and rebuilt. Adjust to the change of a new existence now. Surrender into the new Gaia now. Or it will be very difficult transition. This is a divine decree, and the violation against Gaia will be punished and enacted. Get ready. The time is now. If you all waver, the change and transition will be difficult. Remember that. Choose love, light, peace, joy, and the new beginning. If not the punishment and force of our hand and judgment will be carved into your soul.

Me: Yikes, Divine Mother. Okay, understood. Thank you for the update and messages. It is greatly appreciated, and I'm honored you are trusting me with this info.

Divine Mother: Be well. I/we love you all.

(The day after this transmission, as I was walking my puppy outside, up in the sky there were angels in the sky forming a gold ring. They were banging their swords on their shields. How end times-ish, Divine Mother.)

September 26, 2019

We Are So Screwed

Me: Hi, Archangel Michael. Happy Thursday.

(I smile.)

Archangel Michael: Hi, child. We are the council of light. And we have news.

(I am standing in the middle of a circle, the council surrounding me as bright, powerful columns of gold light. All twelve are there. There are seven triangular stone floor planks in the shape of a pie, carved with runes or symbols into the floor. The ceiling is peaked like the inside of a pyramid.)

Me *(standing in the middle of the circle, right where the metaphoric cherry would be, or dollop of ice cream):* What is the circle?

Archangel Michael: Child. Would you like to hear details of this next phase, the reset protocol?

Me: Yes, please. That'd be great.

Archangel Michael: You all are doing well. We are proud. The integration is going well. The expansion, the rising, the ascending, the inspiring, the teaching, and most importantly, holding the frequency and high vibration is going well. Keep up the good work, the light work, all of you. As for the steps and milestones that will occur next, all of you will integrate and rise, shedding your 3D ego consciousness differently. My/our advice is to surrender, breathe, and allow. If you fight it, it'll be more difficult and take longer. Be ready. We will start the integrations immediately. As for the collective consciousness's death and reset, this will occur on all levels of humanity. The humanity consciousness, the 3D humanity, or collective consciousness will die first. We will disrupt and destroy all the false programming that humanity has been falsely and blindly following, including humanity's ideals of government, leadership, knowledge, truth, systems, culture, religion, beliefs, order, and justice. The human collective will know and see and feel on all levels of their existence the divine truth. They will know, they will see, they will feel, and they will hear the divine truths of all falsehoods and poisoned programming and dark plans or agendas. We/ the council are enacting the reset. First the consciousness, the collective 3D human consciousness, will be destroyed, reset, and rebuilt anew. Then Gaia will be reaped, wiped clean, reset, and rebuilt. Then Gaia will be pieced back together with the fragments that broke from her many, many lost cycles ago. Once she is whole, healed, and rebirthed, she will join the collective, intergalactic community. The humanity program will be no more. This is our decree. Do you understand?

Me: Yes, I believe so. I have a lot of questions but understand I shouldn't have all the answers right away.

Archangel Michael: Yes, that is correct. It will only distract you.

Me: Is the disclosure of the dark agenda and the collapse of everything as we know it a divine truth?

Archangel Michael: Yes, that is a divine truth, one of many. It will be the catalyst, the trigger, and the first of many humanity disasters.

Me: Will that happen on January 12? January 12, 2020?

Archangel Michael: Yes, that is also divine truth.

Me: What about the vision you showed me about the fires, the flood, the ash wiping out, washing, and burning across the West Coast, North and South America, and Canada?

Archangel Michael: Truth, divine truth. That is the second humanity disaster. There will be twelve disasters total to purge, cull, and test humanity. Those who survive, those who ascend or rise, and those who hold the frequency of divine love, light, peace, joy, and hope will ascend into 5D. Those who don't will be reaped, relocated, and sent back to their origins for soul remapping. Do you understand?

(I blink rapidly.)

Me: Yes. It does. Sounds pretty apocalyptic to me. Are there twelve disasters, one a month?

Archangel Michael: Yes, truth. Divine truth.

Me: Oh no. May I ask what kind of disasters? Twelve is a lot.

Archangel Michael: Everything and anything that will shake, rattle, and destroy the false illusions and poisons of 3D programming or existence. They will get progressively worse, each round of humanity disasters. Personal judgment tests were administered this first round, as you call it. Now the collective, global, humanity judgment begins. These are designed to break and awaken the collective to the truth. We are no longer patient or compassionate. We will use whatever mean is necessary to awaken the souls and the collective consciousness to divine truths of existence. The toxicity of 3D has poisoned and diseased Gaia and is staining the other dimensions and intergalactic community. This cannot and will not be. It was left alone for far too long. The end is here. Do you understand?

Me: Yes. Thank you for the update. May I ask a question? I have a few dates that stand out to me, that were told to me. Are they important? February 7? August 25, 2020? A twenty-seventh that's a Saturday?

Archangel Michael: Yes, all are significant. All are collective judgment and disaster days.

Me: If disclosure, flood, and fire are the first tests, what are the other ones?

Archangel Michael: Get ready. All of you. Humanity is falling and resetting. The end is here.

Me: Okay. Thank you for the update. Anything we should be doing?

Archangel Michael: Continue as you are. All of you continue as you are.

Me: This isn't going to be some peaceful or fluffy ascension, is it?

Archangel Michael: It is all perspective. Remain in love, light, peace, and joy and you will pass all the collective humanity disasters. Believe, trust, and surrender. And no, this is not easy. Nor will it be kind. Do you think humanity deserves salvation?

Me: There is still good here. There are still good souls here.

Archangel Michael: That is truth. We will see how those good souls react to collective consciousness judgments, now won't we?

Me: We are so screwed.

September 29, 2019

Time Lines Collapse

Archangel Michael: Surrender and allow. The timelines are collapsing.

Me: Is that why we feel like awful?

Archangel Michael: Yes. Rest and allow.

Me: Is this normal? I keep seeing images absorbing into me.

Archangel Michael: Yes, it's normal. That's all of the *yous* in the incarnation program returning to you as they collapse. Rest and allow. This is normal and nothing to fear. The pressure will ease. Rest.

Me: Okay, Archangel Michael. Thank you. Is this happening to all of us?

Archangel Michael: Yes, child. Rest and allow.

October 4, 2019

Archangel Samael Pays a Visit

(Archangel Samael appears as a white and silver light. We're on the ship. The control room is empty except for me and Archangel Michael and Archangel Samael.)

Archangel Samael: I/we have an update for you.

Me: Sure. Go ahead. Thank you for the update.

Archangel Samael: It is Pluto Season, or as the humans call it, the cycle of death and rebirth. A lot will happen to humanity, Gaia, 3D, and the reality that the 3D collective has built through poisoned programming. As you know, all this will be corrected and reset. I am here to give you all an update on the upcoming reaping cycle and subsequent judgments.

Me: Okay. Please continue.

Archangel Samael: The first wave of destruction and judgment will be to the dark and elite. Their jurisdiction and overthrow of 3D collective consciousness is now complete. Their punishment and destruction will set Gaia and humanity on a path of necessary ascension. There will be two additional waves of reapings. The second wave will reap the gray souls. How painful, how traumatic, how gentle, how kind, and how fair it is will be up to the destroyers.

Me: Please define what a reaping is.

Archangel Samael: Destruction of the 3D, physical vessel, unplugging of the consciousness from the 3D programming, and returning the soul back to its origin location or reassignment for more soul work. The light will ascend to power 5D. The gray's judged and weighed. The dark is destroyed, returned to source.

Me: Thank You for clarifying. What do you want us to do? This part we were previewed already. Any other details to share? Timing, etc.?

Archangel Samael: The first wave is and will be as originally plotted, before your human end of calendar year (Mayan).

Me: When is the end of the Mayan calendar?

Archangel Samael: Specific human time is irrelevant. It is a false construct created to enslave 3D collective and humanity. The only measure of accuracy is your universal planets, stars, and lunar and solar alignments. They will give you all an indicator of when the waves will be.

Me: What about the dates given?

- Dec 2019: First reaping
- January 2020: First global disaster—ring of fire shifts and erupts, unearthing an ancient city
- December 2020ish: Second reaping
- 2021/2022: End game. 3D is gone.

Archangel Samael: Yes, those are divine truths. And yes those are the end times and reset protocol. For accuracy and specifics, if that is what you all need, follow the planetary alignments with the moon and sun and look for the anomalies. These are your clues. The plan and decree is in motion.

Me: And there is no changing your mind? There isn't a chance this can be undone?

Archangel Samael: No. This is for the betterment of Gaia and all. Remember, Gaia is the priority above all else. She is the epicenter of a much larger intergalactic ecosystem.

Me: Okay. What do you want us to do? Doesn't seem like there is much to do.

Archangel Samael: For now, continue as you all are. Remember to hold the frequency and vibration of your highest expression and that of divine love, light, peace, and joy.

Archangel Samael: This is merely a check-in and a test to see if you all are wavering or stand firm in this truth. I say this because wavering will not lead to a fate and timeline where an end times protocol doesn't exist. Wavering will lead to a lower vibration or frequency where end times impact the soul and carry traumas. The way to enlightenment and ascension is through the pain, discomfort, change, and rebirthing of humanity, Gaia, and self or consciousness. Do you understand? All timelines and fate lines at this juncture end with the dying of Gai. This is why the destroyer reset protocol has been activated, because Gaia must be saved. Do not waver, as the way to enlightenment ad ascension is through the pain of rebirth. Humanity is being given opportunities to rebirth itself. Those who surrender and adapt to change will pass and ascend. Those who resist will struggle, and it will not go well on their soul judgment. Understand.

Me: Yes, thank you.

Archangel Samael: Continue as you are, as all of you are. You all are doing well. The rebirth of the collective will be painful, uncomfortable, and at most times dark. We will bring humanity to its knees so they may awaken. Pain is oftentimes the greatest lesson. Remain in love, light, peace, and joy and you all will prosper and be free of the 3D collective very, very soon.

Me: Thank you for the message and insights. We are grateful. Is there anything else?

Archangel Samael: Just that I/we love you. What we do is because of love, and only love. Breathe and remain centered. Know that everything is not always as it seems, as your collective mind perceives it to be. Be patient. Trust. And know that divine love, light, peace, and joy are already there for you all. Trust, believe, and breathe.

Me: Thank you for the messages.

October 6, 2019

Stop Fighting the Integration

Archangel Michael: Stop fighting the integration collective. All you have to do is breathe. Stop resisting.

Me: What exactly is happening? Stop resisting what exactly?

Archangel Michael: Just breathe. All will be well.

M.V.RAYHN

October 11, 2019

Archangel Samael Pep Talk

Stop thinking.
Start feeling.

October 16, 2019

Dark Nights of the Soul Strengthen Us

Archangel Michael: You all endure soul trials to strengthen you. No one, nothing, and no event can harm or enslave you all unless you choose and agree to these circumstances. You are always safe, protected, shielded, and blessed by the divine. Nothing will ever harm you all.

November 1, 2019

This Is Ascension

Archangel Michael: Good job. Good job with everything you all have done to ascend out of 3D. We are all very impressed. *(He smiles.)* You all are exceptional. Lead and help the others ascend as well. You are all on separate paths of ascension. Awaken parts of your shadowed soul that need to be healed and integrated. You all are transitioning to another plane and dimension. You are not exiting all of existence, just the 3D matrix.

Me: Is that what's happening to this physical vessel? This human coil?

Archangel Michael *(He looks at me):* Do you think you all are ready for that knowledge? Do not fear. Do not fear this. We will help you all through this. It is not as scary as your human mind perceives it to be. This is ascension. This will be happening to all of those ascending into 5D. You all will not be alone.

Me: So does that mean a large number of 3D humans will ascend into 5D and their 3D human vessels are going to be found on the 3D ground?

Archangel Michael: Don't worry about the details. The objective is to release you all from 3D enslavement and not create more trauma. All will be well. You will see.

Higher Me *(smiles):* This is the collective's ascension path. This is what everyone has been working hard for. This is what everyone has been healing their soul traumas for. This is why you all have looked at all of your shadows and soul traumas—for healing, for transmuting, for ascending your soul into 5D and out of the matrix. Remember, 3D is not real. It is a consciousness simulation program that has been compromised by the dark. We, the collective, *want* to leave. Your mission all along was to enter the corrupt program. Heal yourselves. Discover ways to break out of the matrix and system and ascend *out*. Enter. Assess. Heal. Ascend. That was your mission.

November 6, 2019

Do Not Forget the Simple Joys

Archangel Michael: You are all doing well on your paths to 5D ascension, and you all will rise out of 3D/4D right as planned. We are very proud of all your feats. You all have exceeded our expectations.

Archangel Michael: We want you all to rest and take some time to enjoy life a little. While you all are rising, ascending, and rebirthing yourselves into a new existence or dimension far ahead of our expectations, do not forget the simple joys of things, of existence, of life, of 3D/4D. Nothing is wrong with you all. You are safe. It was to help you. Your fatigue and human symptoms are all side effects from the reintegrations with source.

(He smiles.)

Archangel Michael: You all will feel better soon. Give all of your selves time to adjust, acclimate, and orient with the new you—the new energy signature or flow and the new existence. More abilities will emerge. Do not be alarmed by this. You all are doing very well. I am very proud of you all.

November 13, 2019

Humanness Slowly Ends

Me: What's going to happen, Archangel Michael?

Archangel Michael: The end times protocol. I told you last year that everything, everyone, every place, and every event, including you all, including 3D and all its timelines, realities, frequencies, vibrations, and dimensions would end. Humanity will feel body, mind, spirit, and soul on all of their levels end times and the reset. Those who are worthy will ascend. Those in the gray will be reaped, judged, weighed, and reset to new destinations or sent home. The dark will be punished and destroyed. The end times are here and in motion.

Me: How long is this going to take to manifest in this timeline or collective consciousness or 3D/4D?

Archangel Michael: Patience. The plan we gave you all stands firm. The earth, 3D, reality, and existence as you all know will cease to exist. Change, the reset, the rehabilitation, the ascension, and the separation now begin. All of you will ascend. You all will not have to fear. You all are always safe. You all will begin to see and experience large-scale global and collective shifts. Everyone, everything, every place, every event, every reality, every timeline, every frequency, and every vibration will shift. You will all begin to see splits and polarities and bifurcations. It is unstoppable. Surrender to it. These changes are now beyond all of your control. Continue on as you all have. But you will all begin shifting into your higher selves and into your soul and mission roles. The soul is the true reason you all are here. Your humanness will die, and your human reality will die. Step into your divine roles and begin. Do not fight the change or you all will feel the pain. Surrender into trust and all will be well. The end times protocol begins.

Me: Okay, thank you, Archangel Michael. Anything else? Can I stop going to work now? Ha, ha. And spend my days in joy?

Archangel Michael: You all will. There will no longer be an enslavement program. Be patient and watch it crumble. You all will know when it is time to walk away from humanness. You will all know. We along with the divine will help and guide you all. Do not fear. Remember that.

Me: Okay, Archangel Michael. Thank you.

Archangel Michael: Job well done. I'm proud of you all. Rest. Don't overthink the mundane. It will all change and end. Receive all of your well-deserved blessings. You all have worked hard. A new beginning. A new earth. A new Gaia is here.

Me: Yay!

November 14, 2019

The Exit

Me: I am ready for the divine truth. Please provide more details. I am ready, Archangel Michael. I'm ready for it. Please help.

(I'm on the ship standing next to Archangel Michael, who looks at me sideways, hands behind his back casually.)

Archangel Michael: Do you want this knowledge? You have a choice.

(He looks at me pointedly but with warm eyes.)

Archangel Michael: You all have come a long way since one human year ago. You all have surpassed your soul lessons, tests, trials, and trainings. Do I think you are ready for this divine truth? Yes. Remember, do not be afraid.

Me: Okay, I won't. Okay, I trust you. Hit me with the truth, Archangel Michael.

Archangel Michael: Remember when I said the original plan still stands?

Me: Yes. I thought there were waves of reapings. Not all human souls would perish at the same time.

Archangel Michael: Yes, that is still divine truth. Remember I said do not be afraid?

Me: I'm not afraid, surprisingly. I'm very at peace with the whole thing. I'm neutral about it.

(He looks at me pointedly.)

Archangel Michael: I/we will never, ever hurt you all out of ill intent. You all already know to approach this with your expanded nonhuman consciousness. Your awareness and your 3D memories will live on and be integrated. You all will be and feel whole again, integrated and whole with all your selves and source. There is nothing to fear. Trust. All will be well.

Me: May I request it be gentle and painless and peaceful?

Archangel Michael: You all will feel as if you've returned home. You all will feel the unconditional love of source, of the divine, of peace, of joy, of love, and of light.

Me: I'm sorry, my human mind likes details. Last year I received messages and visions of my vessel just collapsing and I rose up out of the body permanently. Is that truth?

Archangel Michael: Yes, it is. All of humanity will fall. The destroyers will be the first, as the architects and leaders of the reapings.

Me: I'm sorry, what happened to the exploding volcanoes and ring of fire and shifting plates and tow-trucking Gaia back and the merkaba and all of that? I believe you said by 2021 to 2022 Gaia will be reaped and fully reset. 3D will no longer be? I'm so confused.

Divine Mother: Child.

Me: Divine Mother?

(Everyone in the control room of the ship knelt in reverence, heads down. That's how you know the Divine Mother is one bad ass boss lady.)

Divine Mother: Do not be afraid. What I revealed to you all is divine truth, decreed and most importantly soul mapped by you all. This was and is part of the end times plan that was approved by me and the council. Do not be afraid. Think beyond the human ego mind. Think and transcend the human ego mind beyond human fear of death. You all are not dying. You all are returning home and exiting a false program that has enslaved you all for far too long and for far too many cycles. The end is here for the dark.

Me: So the twelve volcanoes erupting, Lemuria rising, and all that— is *that* still happening?

Archangel Michael: Yes it is. That is all divine truth and the divine end times plan. That still stands.

Me: And the three waves of reapings? Dark, gray, light? Over the course of one human year-ish?

Archangel Michael: Yes, the reapings will occur in stages by frequency of soul. Frontline destroyers first, frontline, then dark, gray, and light. There will be some special cases that will be in the earlier or later stages, but that detail is unnecessary. Some may stay behind, as their souls choose, but all souls by the completion of end times will be reaped from Gaia, and 3D, 2D, and 1D will be destroyed. 4D will remain for transitioning souls into 5D. All will be well. You all will know when to abandon humanness. A global and collective event will introduce global and collective chaos, and your human work will be no more.

Me: Okay. Well wow.

Archangel Michael: Breathe. And do not be afraid. More to come. Breathe.

November 15, 2019

You Are Coming Home

Divine Mother: I know we have given you all a big burden to bear
for your human and nonhuman selves. It is because we know the
strength in your soul, your spirit, your mind, and your body. But
rest easy and be at peace that what is to come is not to be feared.
It is necessary for the end times protocol and most importantly
for you all. It will bring you all that much closer to source, your
highest self, and all your selves, and you all will feel better. You
all will be home with us and you will finally feel peace. I/we
know and see the pain and hurt and loneliness in your souls.
But know that it is temporary and you all will be with us. You
will feel like yourself very, very soon.

November 25, 2019

Choosing 5D

Archangel Michael: Congratulations collective. You all are doing well. You continue to choose 5D and ascension out of 3D. I/ we know it is not easy. I know this and sympathize. You are all strong, stronger than all of us. We are so proud of you all. Continue rising. Continue shedding your humanness and 3D programming. The more you shed, the more you step into 5D and higher and break through the veil. The more you all step away from 3D ego consciousness programming, the more you begin to see, hear, and feel the divine truth of the corrupt 3D matrix and rise and ascend to who you all really are and the divine truth of everyone, everything, every place, and every event that has been corrupted by the dark. You are all transitioning into 5D, your divine, true self, and your soul mission or purpose. This will be uncomfortable, and you all will feel in-between dimensions imbalances often. But just remember to honor your mind, body, spirit, and soul and you all will quickly adjust. I am so proud.

Me: Thank you for the message.

M.V.RAYHN

December 2, 2019

All Will Be Well

Archangel Michael: Just breathe. All will be well. You all are blessed and supported by the divine always. Whatever your heart desires, it will be blessed and it will be so. Rest easy. This doesn't matter. None of this matters anymore. Follow your soul. We will help you all no matter what. Stand strong in decision, and have no fear. All will be well. You will see. We will align you all to your soul purpose, and you all will never be without. I/we are proud of you all for finally being at peace and learning that your mind, body, spirit, and soul come before external factors. Rise and ascend out of the matrix. Rise and inspire others to do the same. I/we love you all and know that you will always be blessed and abundant. Rest. And be at ease. All will be well.

December 5, 2019

All Paths Manifested Are Joy

Divine Mother: You are all ready for the divine truth now and are becoming stronger each day, each moment, each breath. You are all becoming your true self and shedding your 3D programming, identity, and ego mind. You are becoming you. I want you all to play. Play with the magic of the divine and your universal divine energies. You all have not played and surrendered into the loving arms of the divine in too long of a time. Surrender and trust in the divine and her universal magic and let her lead you all to your soul purpose and new self. Be free. Be joyous. Celebrate the magic of living. Play and be grateful and happy. Cast your worries aside. Your human needs will be taken care of. You all will always be cared for and supported by the divine. Release this unwarranted fear and be free. You are all free of 3D. You are now creating magic with the divine. Allow her to show you the blessings and abundance and the paths to joy and ascension. You all deserve this freedom. It is time for you all to unshackle yourself from 3D enslavement and false programming. Step into ascension and freedom. You all have earned it. I am so proud of everything you all have done to get to this moment. I am so proud and love you all very much. I love all my children very much. Be joyous and free.

Me: Thank you, Divine Mother. What should we do now?

Divine Mother: Be free. That is all. The end times are already underway. Focus on ascension now. The end times. The reapings. The reset. You all will know when that time is near. Joy is your assignment now. Your responsibilities can wait a breath while

93

you all enjoy the remnants of 3D. There will be plenty to do. Worry not of that now. For now be free.

Me: Thank you, Divine Mother. I love you.

Divine Mother: I love you too. Rest now. Your burdens are no more.

December 9, 2019

We Cannot Ascend into 5D with Only Two Strands of DNA

Archangel Michael:

- Finish the message. Finish the paragraph. The sentence at the end is the answer. It is the sentence that goes into the DNA strand, that goes into the brain.
- We are building DNA in all of you. Each sentence is building a DNA strand.
- Eventually you will receive a paragraph revealed with instructions.
- These instructions will be how to ascend.
- We have been implanting this whole year, with these messages.

December 18, 2019

I Am the Sun

Divine Mother: I am all things, and all things are me. What you refer to as the central sun is me. And I am the central sun. But if your human mind needs an explanation. It is because I have not yet fully integrated with all of the *mes* as of yet. I am … experiencing. *(She smiles.)*

Me *(I smile)*: I'm honored you're with me and grateful to be experiencing with you.

Divine Mother: When the time is right, I will set you all free to return home—to return to paradise how it should have been and to return to yourselves and your loved ones. I will free all my children and punish those who have dared to corrupt the beauty of existence. All will know. For now, just be. Live freely and be happy. You all are free now.

Me: Thank you. *(I smile.)*

December 24, 2019

The Creators

(Divine Mother shows me a blue energy, divine masculine, and a pink energy, divine feminine, and they create a ball of white and gold light. From that white and gold light they created everything—millions and millions of little gold lights dispersed into people, things, places, and events.)

Me: We are one of those dots? That I can understand.

(Divine Mother shows me a rainbow of colors, twelve altogether. Each is a different color.)

Me: Are those the archangels? I thought they created everything.

Divine Mother: They did. *(She shows me how the twelve archangels would take a gold/white ball of light and mold and create it into something. They did so with all the millions and millions of gold/white dots.)*

Me: So the little gold/white lights are unformed balls of energy, and the archangels used that to make stuff? Okay. Got that. Thank you for the information. What do we do now?

Divine Mother: You have done enough. It is time to rest. *(She boops me on the nose.)* Better days and moments will arise.

Me: Thank you, Divine Mother.

December 25, 2019

End Times Are Everywhere

Me: What is going on?

Archangel Michael *(standing casually with arms behind his back)*: The Divine Mother happened … that's what is going on. *(He's amused.)* End times, child. End times. *(Sighs.)* I can't say I'm not relieved. This was a long time in coming.

Me: Divine Mother?

(I feel her sit on the bed.)

Divine Mother: Just be for now. There is nothing for you all to do. You are all safe, and you are all free. No one, thing, place, or event will ever harm you all … ever. This took a lot of planning and pain and trauma and tears on all of our parts. But all is well now, and we are free. We are all free. And the injustice will be paid and punished twofold and the evil corruption and darkness eliminated and destroyed for good. End times are here, child, and it is time the corruption is addressed and balance is restored. It has gone long enough.

Me: Does that include 3D?

Divine Mother: It *begins* in 3D. You all have already helped and cleared the way by eliminating the darkness at the creator level. The darkness had poisoned existence so much it had reached our brothers and sisters. We are the original creators and destroyers of all. We cannot be corrupted. Our souls must be pure. It's been some time since that was divine truth. *(She smiles.)* It's time to rest and begin anew. You all will have the choice of where to go once the mission is complete. It will be laborious, but it will be done. It is a new beginning for us all.

Me: I just know the way 3D is now … it's not sustainable. Something has to change.

Divine Mother: Whatever your soul desires, it will be so. You are all safe and you are all well. All of the yous—this was needed for you all to rebirth yourself and begin anew, whole, complete, healed, unbound, free to be as you are and as the Divine Mother and Divine Father intended. As source intended. There were those who were afraid of you all and kept you shackled and repressed. But you all are free now. And we will show them all what happens when they hurt my babies.

Me: We missed you … very much. Are you going to clean house and kick everyone's ass?

Divine Mother: We will do more than that … much more than that. *(She smiles.)* Now the work begins. End times are already underway. You all will begin to see much-needed changes and beginnings for 3D. Also remember that Gaia must still be healed. Just be for now and watch an end to darkness, evil, and corruption begin.

Me: Should we do anything?

Divine Mother: Just rest and be. Just rest and be.

December 26, 2019

The Grand Council of Light and Archangels

The higher we ascend, the clearer we *see*. Whereas before, people, places, things, and events seemed blurry and fogy, now when my spirit travels (which can be done with ease while I am conscious), there is a crispness.

Turns out the grand council of light (a.k.a., *the* archangels) resemble what the Egyptians knew to be divine truths all along. They have human bodies with animal heads. Of course, these higher dimensional beings, and the original twelve creators of everyone, everything, every place, and every event, have multiple guises and take many shapes and personas.

January 2, 2020

You Are All Safe … Always

Divine Mother: I have been watching and watch over you all as I always do. You all are doing so incredibly well. Continue on as you are, rising out of the toxic 3D matrix, back into the galactic multiverse center to a higher dimension, frequency, and vibration of light. Remember to be safe and that you are all always safe. Always. I, your father, will always watch over you all. Always. You all and my creations will be healed very soon, and you all will return home. The divine light and divine feminine is here and will eradicate, erase, and destroy the dark and reset that which is wrong and make it right again. Do not fear what is coming and what will happen. It is decreed and divinely guided. You all and those who are worthy, those who are vibrating high enough to absorb change, will ascend and rise and return and step out of the false, poisoned matrix. Those who are unawakened, trapped within their karma, their judgment, their low, confused frequency, will remain there. They will be reaped and reassigned. All else, everyone, everything, every place, and every event responsible for hurting my Gaia and my program and my creations made with love and light and joy will suffer a very painful price. Once all the souls are free, a judgment and destruction will be enacted on all those responsible. Their souls and everyone, everything, every place, and every event from whence they came and ever were and ever will be, will be no more, ever, ever again. I will erase them from existence for being a stain, cancer, and poison in our existence and this and all intergalactic multiverses. For now stay close with your sisters and continue being open to the divine light messages we/I am sending you all. You are all doing well.

(She smiles.)

Divine Mother: You are all safe. Remember, you will all be safe through the reset protocol and end times protocol and rehabilitation protocol. Remember that always. We led you all to information because it is important information and an example and preview of what is to come and the darkness that has put all of you in the stronghold of the 3D, dark matrix enslavement. It will be no more. My patience is no more, and my wrath at the imbalance and injustice will be unleashed. No one, nothing, no place, no event, no evil, no darkness, and no negativity will continue harming any and all creations of divine love light and joy. I/we will not tolerate it. Remember, you are all safe and divinely protected by love, light, joy, and the infinite source of light always. You all are our warriors of light and are divinely safe, protected, and shielded always. Destruction is not a mal-intended, dark, evil-rooted protocol. Destruction and death are necessary to heal, rebirth, and begin anew. Do not fear the change and destruction that are coming and have already begun. It is necessary for Gaia, my Gaia, and for humanity and the souls trapped in that matrix to return and remember the infinite source of light and love they are and the bountiful, beautiful, connected consciousness of divine love, light, peace, and joy they all are. I love all of you. Remember, you are all safe always. Always. You all will return home soon. Be patient for just a little longer.

January 2, 2020

Humans Even Messed Up God *and* Goddess

Archangel Michael: Divine Father is what humans refer to as God. He is *the* energy of all and everything. Like us all. We are all many things all at the same time. But in simple human terms … yes, he is God. Divine Father and Divine Mother are both God. Understand?

Me: Why does he/she want to talk to me? I'm just a dot—a peon.

Archangel Michael: Why not talk to you? He/she/they speak to everyone and everything. They are everyone and everything. Humans have even found a way to screw up something as simple as communing with the divine. They/God/source is in all of us in *all* things. It is easy to commune with them. They are us. We are them.

Me: Well, if you put it like that …

Archangel Michael: He/they confirmed for you all what you already knew. He/she/they have not changed their mind or decree. End times are upon us all, everywhere, anywhere, and in between.

Me: Oh. Okay. Great. Good times. Did it happen already?

Archangel Michael: You think it happened already?

Me: I know you can freeze time and fix things and make it seem like it never happened. I was just curious.

Archangel Michael: It's begun. It's nowhere near finished. It will be a long and difficult journey for us all.

January 14, 2020

We Are the Sword

The mission that *we*, as the collective, have:

1. Save Gaia.
2. Save humanity. Set humanity free.

We are the *sword*.

When we *all* integrate and unite *together*, we *become* the sword.

We are God's sword—the end to the chaos.

CHAPTER 5

Hello.

I *Am* God and Goddess.

January 18, 2020

Who and What Is the Real Goddess/God?

Divine Mother: God, who is pure love, wouldn't manipulate. God is *love*. God isn't an entity but pure love energy. So whoever claims to be "God" is a false prophet. Humans continue to misunderstand God. It is an energy of love and light. It doesn't need praying or worshiping to. It is in all of us. It is our jobs to make humanity aware of their false beliefs as this is feeding the false prophets and evil. All you have to do is believe and manifest from the heart and soul anything the soul desires and it will be. Humanity's mistake is giving their power away to false prophets and evil. You don't need to pray or beg or ask. You create from the soul as our souls are all infinite sources of love and light. We all have that power to create. We don't need permission from anyone. Do you understand?

Believe in good.
Believe in love.
Believe in light.
Believe in peace.
Believe in joy.
Believe *you* have the power to create.
That is all.

And most importantly, *believe* the truth and knowledge in your soul. I/we love you all. You all are doing very well and uncovering divine truths humanity needs to understand and learn.

Me: Thank you, Divine Mother.

February 3, 2020

A Message in Dreams

God/Goddess: My kingdom is your kingdom.

February 7, 2020

Consciousness Death …

God/Goddess: You all are already part of a *new*, reprogrammed collective, one remade with and from *light* and *God*/Goddess.

Me: Are we dead already? Is this the afterlife?

God/Goddess: No, it is still the experience you are manifesting and cocreating your reality. You will, what you call, cross over to the macro reality. Until then, your soul is not yet finished with the mission and will continue manifesting and creating your 3D, 4D, or 5D micro reality until your soul mission is complete. Your/our soul will dictate when that end is. For now, *be*. Enjoy the journey and freedom from the toxic consciousness poisoning 3D.

Me: Did everyone in 3D/4D cross over to this new, reprogrammed collective consciousness?

God/Goddess: I/we think you know the answer to that. *All* souls will eventually transfer to the new collective consciousness. The question is *when*. It will be when their souls are ready and their consciousness *remembers* and *awakens*. This cannot be forced but must occur organically. When they are ready, they will shift to the new consciousness. The closer they become to *me/we/us*, the closer they become to breaking their false reality and awakening. Continue and keep on your path.

February 8, 2020

Pay Attention

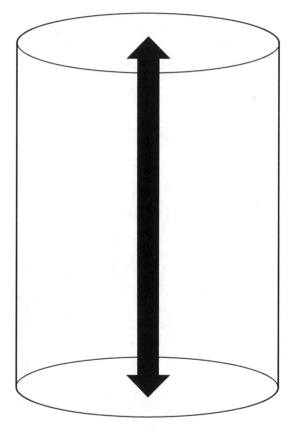

Two Way
Singular and Multiversic Gateway

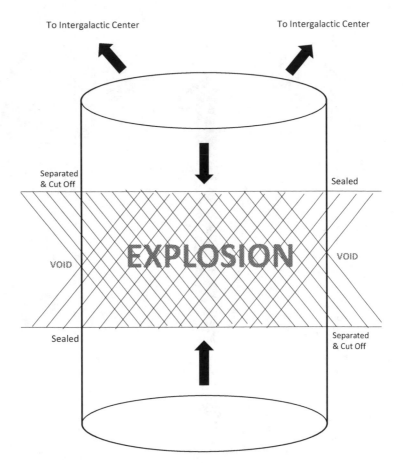

5D + Other Dimensions

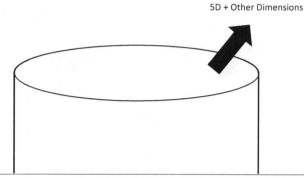

Repaired Torus Field

The 12 DNA Strands allow us to jump this Torus Field

12 DNA = Quantum Leaping Ability & Return to <u>God</u>

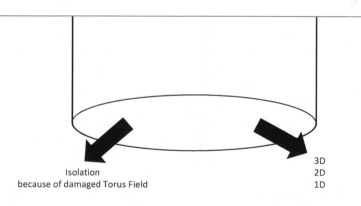

Isolation
because of damaged Torus Field

3D
2D
1D

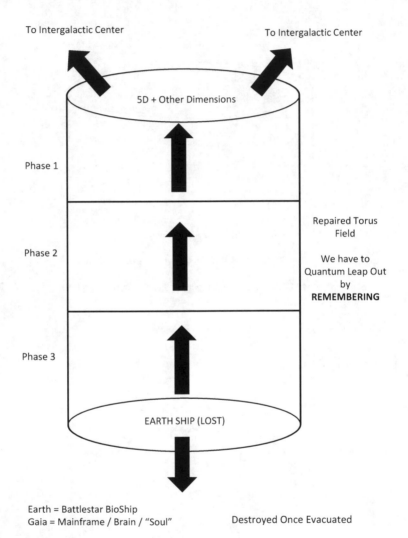

To Intergalactic Center

To Intergalactic Center

5D + Other Dimensions

Phase 1

Phase 2

Repaired Torus Field

We have to Quantum Leap Out by **REMEMBERING**

Phase 3

EARTH SHIP (LOST)

Earth = Battlestar BioShip
Gaia = Mainframe / Brain / "Soul"

Destroyed Once Evacuated

February 8, 2020

Earth Is a BioShip

God/Goddess: Earth's quantum leap functionality was damaged in the war and destruction of the what we can call universal hemispheric membrane and for lack of a human term, a nucleus, which plugged her into the intergalactic centralized ecosystem and heart, brain, and power. The unity collective is *godhead* energy power. She has been lost and offline for too long. The souls on board have been lost and away for too long. They have been asleep for so long that they've forgotten that they are not part of the intergalactic community. Help them awaken and rise.

Me: Really!

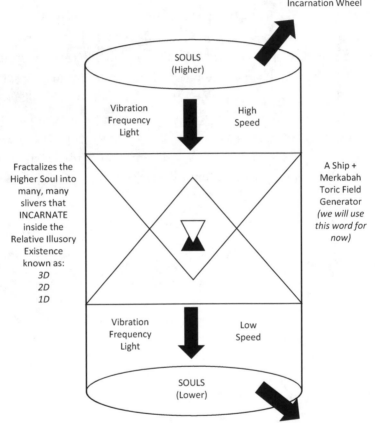

Absolute Truth Existence /
Incarnation Wheel

SOULS
(Higher)

Vibration
Frequency
Light

High
Speed

Fractalizes the
Higher Soul into
many, many
slivers that
INCARNATE
inside the
Relative Illusory
Existence
known as:
3D
2D
1D

A Ship +
Merkabah
Toric Field
Generator
*(we will use
this word for
now)*

Vibration
Frequency
Light

Low
Speed

SOULS
(Lower)

Relative Illusory Existence /
Incarnation Wheel

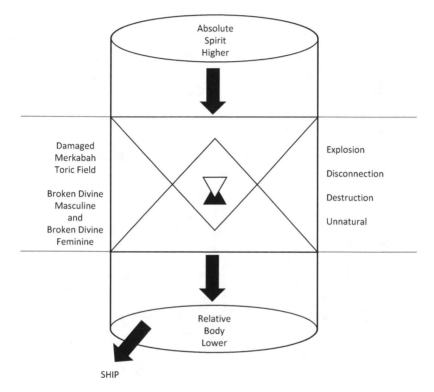

SHIP = Soul. Halves. In. Progress

February 8, 2020

SHIP: Soul Halves In Progress

God/Goddess:

- Incarnating souls
- Experiencing defractilized souls
- Because of damaged Merkabahic toric generation field
- Defractilized souls cannot fractilize and return to the higher self or over soul.
- The relative illusory existence of human avatar suits have been malfunctioning and cannot power up, logicalize, and reconnect with higher self or soul intelligence (humans call it DNA) to disconnect from the human avatar suit and return to higher self/higher soul.
- The only way out and to rejoin or reintegrate the soul fractalized pieces is through spirit, leaving the avatar behind and *remembering* to *return* to higher self, higher soul, and godhead oversoul.
- The way out is *out of* the avatar suit—literally *through* spiritual and soul *remembrance.*
- Remembering activates the soul tether and reconnects past the Merkabahic toric field. It is too damaged to fix fully. It's a Band-Aid, we may call it.

God/Goddess: Rest for now. This is a lot to take in. We will continue again.

Me: Thank you for the message and information.

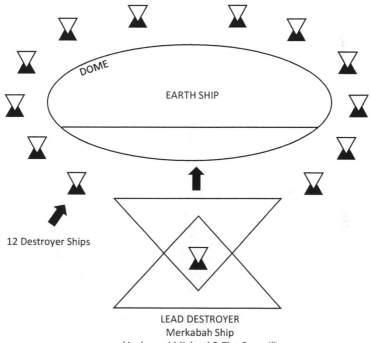

DOME

EARTH SHIP

12 Destroyer Ships

LEAD DESTROYER
Merkabah Ship
(Archangel Michael & The Council)

February 9, 2020

Recreating a Quantum Toric Hemispheric Dimensional Jump Field

God/Goddess:

- We need to shift the *earth* ship to its proper dimension and send her home to repair and reset.
- The dimensional jump flare and light speed burn is when the *earth* ship jumps dimension, returning to center.

Me: Thank you for the message.

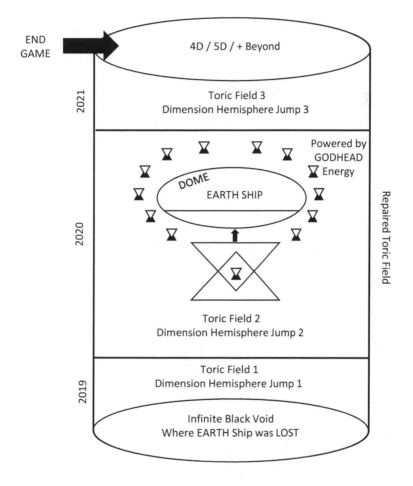

M.V.RAYHN

February 9, 2020

The Cavalry Is Finally Here

God/Goddess: For the centralized membranic toric field to repair, there was a period of waiting until the universe expanded and reexpanded to repair what we will call the web of the membrane field. Travel was not possible until this field was in place. Any and *all* things that tried would disappear and reappear on the other side of the universe. It was a tear in the fabric of my universe. To fix it, we/they/my soldiers had to wait till it repaired itself enough to be stable. Now it is, and that is why the cavalry has arrived. Infinite black voids are the spaces between spaces between the *everything and anything, past the point of dust.* It is void spaces between the absolute truth and relative illusory existences and realities. It is the spaces where I/we/me stretch and expand, create and destroy. It is the equivalent of being stuck in the middle of something being created but not yet. It is an in-between that should be temporary in the creation vibration process and not a permanent place for a large number of our children to be lost and disassociated or disconnected.

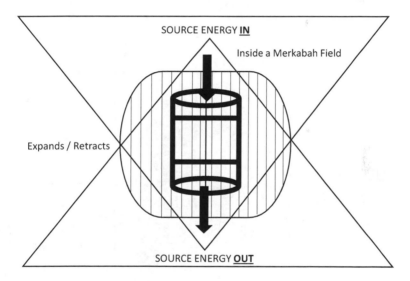

SOURCE ENERGY **IN**

Inside a Merkabah Field

Expands / Retracts

SOURCE ENERGY **OUT**

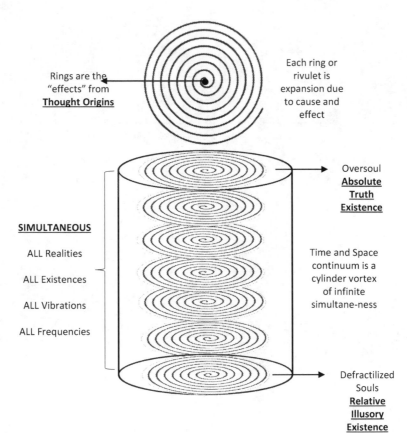

Rings are the "effects" from **Thought Origins**

Each ring or rivulet is expansion due to cause and effect

Oversoul **Absolute Truth Existence**

SIMULTANEOUS

ALL Realities

ALL Existences

ALL Vibrations

ALL Frequencies

Time and Space continuum is a cylinder vortex of infinite simultane-ness

Defractilized Souls **Relative Illusory Existence**

February 10, 2020

Labyrinth (a.k.a., Spacetime Continuum, Where *All* Occurs Simultaneously)

God/Goddess: For the earth ship to ascend and dimensionally jump toric fields one, two, and three, the spacetime continuum and multiple and singular manifestation rings must collapse, creating *space* for the offshoot dimensions, realities, vibrations, and frequencies the *earth ship* has created. These are too important to destroy as they are soul tethered to those onboard. If that soul is still *asleep* and their manifested realties are collapsed, it can do damage to that soul. While all souls are *me/we*, they can still be stained, we shall call it, while in the relative *illusory* world. While all souls cannot cease to exist until I/me/we say, which I/me/we never say, it can take on unnecessary trauma or pain, barring it from learning, growing, and ascending.

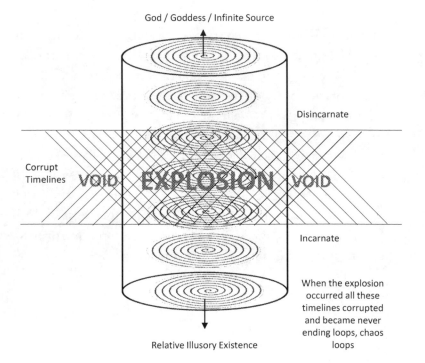

God / Goddess / Infinite Source

Disincarnate

Corrupt Timelines   VOID   EXPLOSION   VOID

Incarnate

When the explosion occurred all these timelines corrupted and became never ending loops, chaos loops

Relative Illusory Existence

God/Goddess: Therefore, these are all timelines that need to be collapsed to repair the toric field and ascend or dimension jump the *earth ship*.

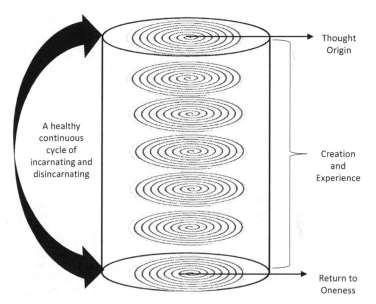

God/Goddess: This model is at the soul level, universe level, galaxy level, and all existence levels. But when the cycle is corrupt or broken, as is the case with the *earth ship, all* souls on board become confused by the disruption in soul creation mechanics.

Absolute Truth Existence / Incarnation Wheel

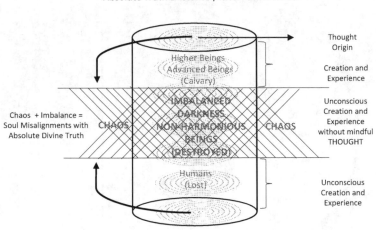

Relative Illusory Existence / Incarnation Wheel

God/Goddess: Stuck. There is no return to the God/Goddess outlet, stuck in patterns of unconscious manifesting, disconnected from soul desire and soul plan.

February 15, 2020

The Gaia Core

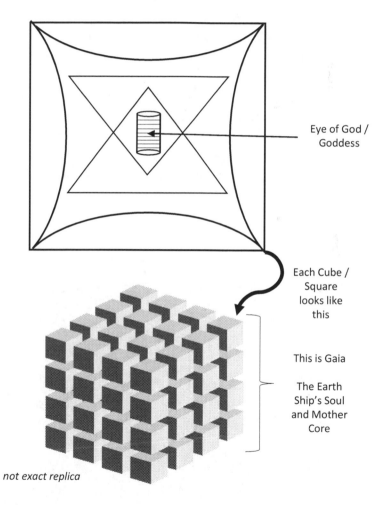

Eye of God / Goddess

Each Cube / Square looks like this

This is Gaia

The Earth Ship's Soul and Mother Core

not exact replica

M.V.RAYHN

February 15, 2020

Godhead-Powered Energy

God/Goddess: All creation is godhead-powered energy, even what humans perceive as technology. All things, people, places, things, and events *are* sentient and alive, because all things are I/we/me. The earth ship is a beautiful creation of our mind, body, and spirit and what humans refer to as advanced, intergalactic, quantum space mechanics. We will use this for now as human minds don't have the vocabulary for it. In the simplest terms, the earth ship is God/Goddess energy and soul fused to machinery to create a thing of beauty. She is natural elements plus technology plus spirit plus magic. It would be easiest if I showed you.

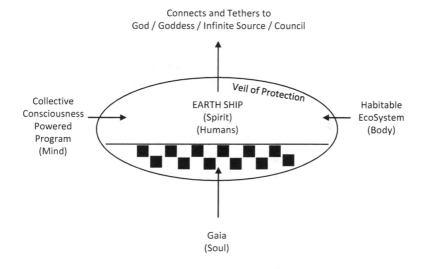

God/Goddess: It's a perfect balance of *mind* (collective consciousness program), *body* (habitable ecosystem), *spirit* (human inhabitants/ avatars), *soul* (godhead energy/power pack), science, and spirituality. They are always *one*.

Me: Are all planets ships?

God/Goddess: Depends. No, not all. There are way too many different types, civilizations, universes, and galaxies for the human mind to comprehend.

February 17, 2020

All Messages Are from God

Archangel Michael: You can safely assume that the messages I/we have given you have been from God/Goddess.

February 18, 2020

Who Are You?

God/Goddess: Just be. You will save humanity and Gaia by just *being*. That is all. Just be. You change others by just being.

February 19, 2020

The Plan

Archangel Michael:

1. Rise, ascend, shed, and transfer (we will call it) to the *new* collective consciousness program.
2. The old collective consciousness (veil) will be terminated.
3. Reap all souls off the earth ship.
4. Judge and evaluate soul maps or plans. Redistribute and relocate them.
5. Settle the 5D-ers (a.k.a., ascended ones).
6. Reset and repair the earth ship and Gaia godhead mainframe.
7. Ascend her off this infinite black void *back* to the intergalactic center.
8. If other souls choose to return to the earth ship, it is of their choosing. It will be repowered, rebuilt, and reequipped with a new Gaia godhead mainframe and mother system.
9. The frontline team is the last to leave.
10. Destroyers are the first to awaken, last to leave. They/we will stay with the earth ship until it is home, back in the intergalactic center.
11. The timeline, as you have already noticed, is speeding up. This is due to the quantum field jumping *over* the corrupt quantum field and timelines. As the earth ship ascends, the timeline will speed up even more.
12. Be prepared for what is to come. You all will use your gifts and talents for this next phase. Awaken and help as many as possible.

February 20, 2020

Absolute Versus Relative

Archangel Michael: Absolute truth is the realm of existence where there is disincarnate, incarnate, fractalized, defractalized, godhead, Christ, manifestation, existence, possibility, actuality, all that is, and all that will ever be, until there is no more, and even then, past the point of dust. There is only singular oneness. This means, in human vernacular, the simultaneousness of everyone, everything, every place, and every event. It transcends time and space. It is the existence of *all*, of *all* people, places, things, and events existing symbiotically, through cause and effect, through the power of creation, through the power of thought energy, through the power of the godhead and Christ energy in us *all*, and in *all* everywhere, anywhere, and in between. It is in this *all*-ness and simultaneousness that absolute truth is.

The absolute truth is that which cannot be altered but exists through very strict natural laws, codes, and rules and predetermined circumstances, sanctioned and dictated by the Divine Mother and Divine Father, Goddess/God, the Almighty. They have created and dictated rules that are unbreakable, as these are the creation and destruction principles that govern all of existence and all of the multiverses *we* all reside in, whether in this dimension, frequency, vibration, reality, speed, space, or time. It is not rules, as human minds understand, as rules in 3D are nonsensical and fabricated from baser ignorance. Rules of the absolute truth universe just *are*, as they *are* existence. They are unbreakable because these rules by Goddess/God dictate the symbiotic mechanics of how any and all things exist together and at the same time.

So when absolute truth is mentioned in this book, in these books, it refers to the existential programming and doctrine that *all* of existence is made of.

As for the relative illusory avatar program, this was put in place for members of the intergalactic community, for souls to expand their experience, their knowledge, their identity, their strength, their weakness, and their tapestry of light, dark, and gray. This program, as that is what it is, is an illusory program put in place as a game for the soul to test itself, to learn about itself, to experience itself, to expand itself, and to ascend itself back to its origin state of perfection. All souls are perfect, as they are all Goddess/God, but when they defractalized and exist separately, at the same time, they are perfectly imperfect. Therefore, they seek to learn, to grow. Like children, they seek adventure, thrill, exploration, fun, and joy, and while obtaining these things, they also discover pain, sadness, and regret. A*ll* of these things, these summations of existing, become soul memories that carry on till there is no more. They become and shape the soul.

In simplest terms, the absolute are a set of fixed doctrine rules that *govern,* while the relative is *illusion.* Understand? Neither is good or bad. They both just *are.* And they both just *are*, together, symbiotically. The soul is created in the absolute, whereas the relative is where it goes to learn. Both are needed for advancement. Both are needed for the soul to expand and to become what it sought to become after leaving source. For at source, *all* things, everyone, everything, every place, and every event is complete and perfect, integrated with godhead creation energy. Soul lessons are complete, and souls have graduated. When a soul returns to source, it leaves the illusory world of the relative, as it has no further need to learn, grow, ascend, and expand.

Of course there are those souls who return to source and the relative, in a continuous, infinite cosmic cycle. And there are those who do so at a limited capacity, their souls fulfilled. And there are those who do both, or other combinations of existing and not. It depends on the soul's choosing.

After the reaping of the earth ship, all souls will have a choice, a *free* will choice, of where to go. They can remain in the illusory world of the relative and be reallocated to another multiverse experience, *or* they can choose to return to source. Neither is wrong. Neither is right. It is up to that soul's choice.

So you see, my child, while humans were taught existence was a mystery, it is, in fact, very simple.

February 21, 2020

The Truth about God/Goddess

Council of Light: I/we/me understand your human mind's frustrations in fully grasping and comprehending the godhead creation energy. The human illusory avatar program is made in such a way where belief is grounded in the physicality of the senses. Seeing is believing, as the human expression goes. Belief. Trust. Faith. While these concepts are oftentimes just words and letters strewn together to represent a feeling or state of being, they, as most of the human language, do not fully convey or express accurately absolute truth. Absolute truth is a knowing, simply put—a knowing of the soul and in the soul. These words, given here by the divine, seek to bridge the gap of understanding and knowing by using human words to reeducate the human avatars here on the earth ship to the truth. This is the truth of what is here, the truth of what is there, in the world of the absolute truth, and the truth in between. Where the earth ship currently resides, in its multiple dimensions, realities, frequencies, vibration off-shoots, and pathways, sits in between the world, the absolute truth, and relative illusion. To truly understand, and to truly remember and ignite the *truth* within one's soul, one has to be remember the truth of existence.

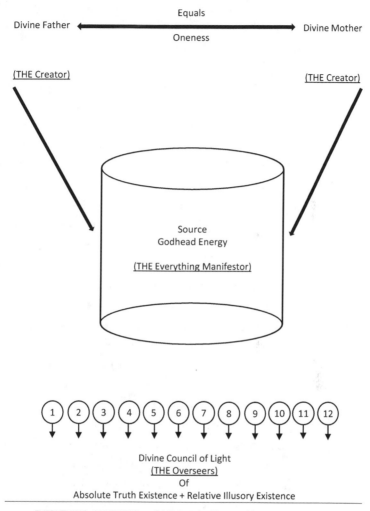

Divine Father ←——— Equals ———→ Divine Mother
Oneness

(THE Creator) (THE Creator)

Source
Godhead Energy

(THE Everything Manifestor)

1 2 3 4 5 6 7 8 9 10 11 12

Divine Council of Light
(THE Overseers)
Of
Absolute Truth Existence + Relative Illusory Existence

EVERYTHING, ANYTHING, and ALL People, Places, Things, Events in Between

Council of Light: So you can see from this image, as that is the best way to communicate complex understanding, with images and feelings, that God and Goddess is a creation energy. It is *all* of us. And *all* of us are them/it. They are not rulers or sovereigns or as humans perceive, a fearful or fear-inducing leader. The godhead is an energy *the* creators use to make manifest any and all things, people, places, and events. One is not higher than the other. One is not lower than the other. They are a balanced system of desire and manifestation. Do you understand?

Me: Yes, sort of. Thank you for the message. It is reprogramming a lot of false human knowledge. Growing up Catholic, we were taught that God is the Almighty, and there is nothing else. He/she is everything, *the* leader, *the* highest there is. Insert here all the verbs and synonyms and the most important thing in the universes and multiverses. If I understand this diagram correctly—and please, correct me—what you're showing me here as God is, for lack of a better human term, and this by *no* means is disrespectful, an energy that is used to create all people, things, places, and events. And the creators use this God energy to create and manifest everything and anything and all people, things, places, and events in between. If my baser human mind is understanding this accurately, creators and "God" are three completely different things. I say three because there is a Divine Feminine Creator, a Divine Masculine Creator and then a "God" source. That is three entities, powers, whatever you want to call it. Am I accurate in saying this?

Council of Light: Yes and no. The creators and godhead energy birthed all at once. They, as a triumvirate, *are* the everything and anything of existence. One cannot exist without the other.

Me: So in that case, if I understand correctly, what humans have been referring to as God is the source energy part of the equation, the Divine Father part of the equation, or the Divine Mother part of the equation. But in absolute truth terms, it is *all three,* a Trinity of absolute truth? Is that what you're saying—that when humans refer to as God is actually Divine Father, Divine Mother, *and* godhead source energy?

Council of Light: Yes, this is divine absolute truth. It is a balanced triumvirate of creation and existence.

Me: So who have we been speaking to this past year and a half, the being that we've been referring to as Divine Mother?

Council of Light: That is the Divine Mother, *the* creator, a corner of the trinity, the triumvirate of creation and existence energy of all that is, and everything and anything. The limited understanding of the human mind, and because of the false programming and corrupt knowledge, absolute truth and knowledge have been lost. And what was circulating in the 3D matrix was only fragmented pieces of truths amalgamated together, creating half-truths and untruths. What humans refer to as God is, to use human arithmetic, a third of a trinity of absolute truth. Do you understand?

Me: Yes, I believe so. I will definitely have more questions after this. When I think of them, may I ask?

Council of Light: Yes, we are here to aid.

Me: Thank you so much. May I ask who you are?

Council of Light: We are the council of light.

Me: Thank you so much for being here and for helping.

Council of Light: We are here to help disseminate absolute truth. We will assist in helping humanity remember the truths of the soul.

February 21, 2020

The Gaia Core Is Dying

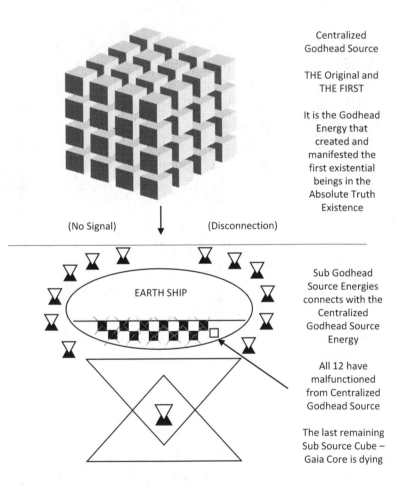

Centralized Godhead Source

THE Original and THE FIRST

It is the Godhead Energy that created and manifested the first existential beings in the Absolute Truth Existence

(No Signal)   (Disconnection)

EARTH SHIP

Sub Godhead Source Energies connects with the Centralized Godhead Source Energy

All 12 have malfunctioned from Centralized Godhead Source

The last remaining Sub Source Cube – Gaia Core is dying

Council of Light: It is extremely critical to repair, reset, and rehabilitate the Gaia core. If she completely dies, the bio earth ship dies along with its inhabitants as the environment and ecosystem will no longer be habitable. There is a small window of possibilities where she doesn't die. And this is why humanity must awaken to stop hurting the Gaia core and earth ship but to also rescue themselves. The earth ship was created by the creators and godhead source as a battle star emergency BioShip for a destroyed planet and civilization due to an intergalactic war that tore that multiverse many billions of light years apart. The inhabitants of the earth ship have been lost in an infinite void, the spaces between spaces, due to the explosive destruction caused by the wars, violence, and advanced weapons that should have never been. The intent of these ships, as there were many when the earth ship was first developed, was to nurture and grow the lost and remaining civilization for when their new planet was ready to inhabit. That planet, a similar one to the one that was destroyed, has been complete and ready for its souls for some time now. Those who have transitioned out of the broken earth ship 3D matrix have transitioned to this new home. They are waiting the rest of their kin. The last and lost inhabitants have been preserved in bio capsules or what human vernacular understands as time-lapsed pods, to preserve and care for the soul that still resides within the vessel.

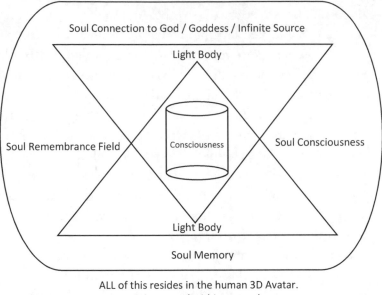

Soul Connection to God / Goddess / Infinite Source
Light Body
Soul Remembrance Field   Consciousness   Soul Consciousness
Light Body
Soul Memory

ALL of this resides in the human 3D Avatar.
It is a vessel within a vessel.
That is what a human suit is.

Council of Light: The human 3D avatar was created to preserve the soul light body, as the origin vessels of these souls were destroyed in the intergalactic war, and destruction was the effect of this devastating war. It was of the utmost importance that these souls were preserved and translocated to safety and new vessels, so that civilization didn't perish. Over the course of translocating to safety and to the newly created planet, the earth ship became lost, for reasons we will discuss at a later time. It was in this infinite black void that it has resided for eons, and it is finally on its way back to where it was destined but never reached. That destination is what humans have been referring to as 5D, paradise, the new garden of Eden, or the new earth. It will no longer be an earth ship but a habitable, balanced, harmonious, symbiotic ecosystem environment.

February 23, 2020

The Akashic and Infinite Source Records

(I am standing beside Archangel Michael, in what appears to be a globe. Inside this globe, in neat rows and columns, are gold symbols and runes. And behind each symbol and rune are other symbols and runes that stretch out infinitely. Wherever it was, it held great power and energy. Just being there and here at the same time was causing my head to be a little dizzy.)

Me: May I ask where we are?

Archangel Michael: These are the original akashic source records. There are many, depending on the universe or galaxy. Each one acts as a epicenter and log of any and all things that occur within that universe or galaxy. Its purpose is so the inhabitants of that universe or galaxy understand the past, present, and future and all in-between dimensions, frequencies, vibrations, realities, and timelines of their civilizations, creations, and manifestations and all the causal effects of those creations and manifestations. *The* absolute divine truth of all existence is the universal law of cause and effect. For every action there is a reaction. For every desire or thought, a creation and manifestation occurs, whether that thought or desire is positive, negative, or neutral. The universal energy and matter that makes up *all* will listen to that request and deliver. It is, to use human vernacular, an on-demand and instant effect and occurrence of people, places, things, and events. Now, whether that creation and manifestation effect *occurs* within your immediate dimension, timeline, frequency, vibration, or reality depends on the individual soul. It may occur instantaneously or lag or even create or manifest an offshoot dimension, timeline, reality, frequency, or vibration. The images we provided earlier show how soul desire and soul trigger work, creating infinite rings and webs of cause and effect loops. For every soul desire and soul trigger, for every singular thought or desire, an outcome is created and manifested. This is for *every* thought and desire. When the thoughts and desires are too negative and create and manifest too many negative offshoot dimensions, realities, timelines, frequencies, and vibrations, it is when that universal system becomes corrupt, as the balance of dark and light, positive and negative, is askew and must be corrected. In that case, and in those cases, the council will step in and eliminate corrupt and toxic timelines, dimensions, realities, frequencies, and vibrations to restore the universal balance. Even though each universe or galaxy is separate, they are *all* interconnected, like a symbiotic web. The source akashic record of each universe or galaxy retains the memory of each timeline, reality, dimension, frequency, and vibration ever created and manifested, along with the origin soul desire and thought. It is, for all intents and purposes, a catalog of each soul in existence or residing in that universe or galaxy and tracks to the most infinitesimal possibility and detail of that soul, individually and collectively. There are many in 3D on the earth ship who can access their universal/galactic akashic record and even their soul records and soul memories. But not many can access *the* original akashic source records. It is here that *all* occurrences of *all* existences since there was no existence are kept. These are the soul memories of the God/Goddess/source membrane and essence. It has the knowledge and wisdom of everything *and* anything that has ever occurred, is occurring, and will occur. It has all possible offshoots, probabilities, and creation or manifestation outcomes. In book two, and others, we will slowly release the origin source knowledge and wisdom that has been lost to humanity and to this universe for eons. It is time the souls on the earth ship remembered the absolute divine truth.

Me: Thank you so much for the message. I have so many questions. I'm not sure where to begin.

Archangel Michael: We will leave it here for now. We will reveal absolute truths differently moving forward. Whereas in book one we used human linguistics, as this is the primary source of communication for humanity, moving forward we will use images and symbols, as these will *implant* within your soul and DNA the keys that will unlock soul memories and soul records. We *all* have access to original akashic source records. It is within *all* of us.

Me: Thank you, Archangel Michael.

Archangel Michael: Be well. More to come. It goes without saying that these symbols should not be manipulated or disseminated unwisely. We have provided these angelic, akashic language, symbols, and codes many times over to humanity, and they have always been corrupted. We will do so once more, through this text, with a warning: they *must* not be tampered with. There will be consequences if they are bastardized.

Me: Yikes. Thank you for the PSA, Archangel Michael.

Archangel Michael: More to come.

Death and Rebirth

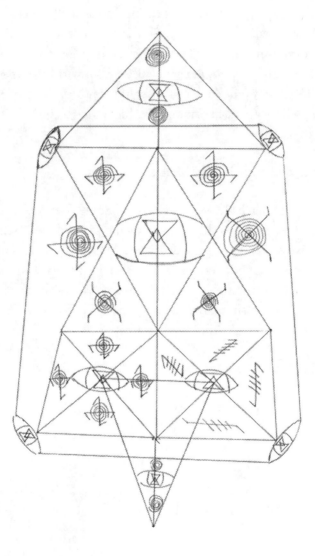

The Eye of Creation

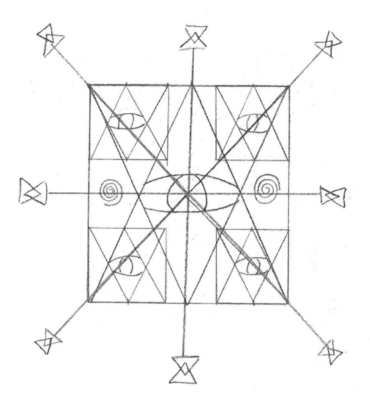

The Divine Father

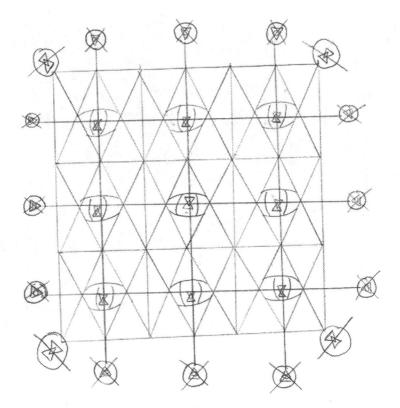

The Divine Mother

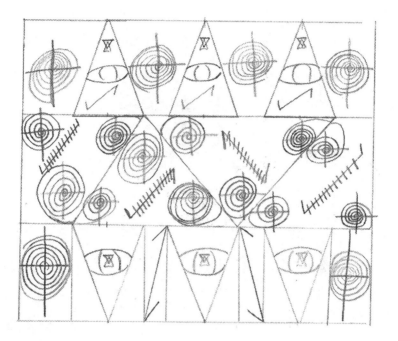

M.V. RAYHN

The Eye of God

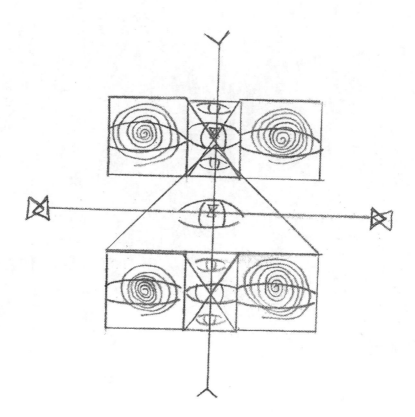

The End of Book One

Me: Does book one end with this?

Archangel Michael: You have enough for book one. You may put it out as is. It is complete. We will assist with disseminating it to all of humanity, those unawakened, who need to remember. They must remember who they really are to return to divine love, light, peace, and joy. The awakened will usher in the end times. It will be the end of the fear, darkness, poison, and corruption that have gone on for way too long, killing our Gaia and spreading cancer across the multiverse. It is time for 3D humanity to rise and up and awaken to usher in and bring in the new earth. Thank You for being our pen and voice of the divine.

Me: Is this enough information?

Archangel Michael: This is enough for book one. As it is, it's a lot. Remember, this is not just a book but a building of DNA and reprogramming of the soul map. Too much all at once will overwhelm.

(I smile.)

Me: Thank you for gifting me with the honor of being the vehicle to deliver these important messages.

Archangel Michael: Be in peace. Be in love. Be in light.

ABOUT THE AUTHOR

M. V. Rayhn scribes messages of infinite love and light and continues the journey of soul remembrance, balancing being of service, uncovering absolute divine truths, and experiencing mundane joys. She currently lives in the New York City area.

Printed in the United States
By Bookmasters